Cambridge Elements

Elements in Gender and Politics
edited by
Tiffany D. Barnes
University of Kentucky
Diana Z. O'Brien
Washington University in St. Louis

COUNTER-STEREOTYPES AND ATTITUDES TOWARD GENDER AND LGBTQ EQUALITY

Jae-Hee Jung
University of Houston
Margit Tavits
Washington University in St. Louis

CAMBRIDGE
UNIVERSITY PRESS

Shaftesbury Road, Cambridge CB2 8EA, United Kingdom

One Liberty Plaza, 20th Floor, New York, NY 10006, USA

477 Williamstown Road, Port Melbourne, VIC 3207, Australia

314–321, 3rd Floor, Plot 3, Splendor Forum, Jasola District Centre, New Delhi – 110025, India

103 Penang Road, #05–06/07, Visioncrest Commercial, Singapore 238467

Cambridge University Press is part of Cambridge University Press & Assessment, a department of the University of Cambridge.

We share the University's mission to contribute to society through the pursuit of education, learning and research at the highest international levels of excellence.

www.cambridge.org
Information on this title: www.cambridge.org/9781009462655

DOI: 10.1017/9781009406628

When citing this work, please include a reference to the DOI 10.1017/9781009406628

First published 2024

A catalogue record for this publication is available from the British Library.

ISBN 978-1-009-46265-5 Hardback
ISBN 978-1-009-40665-9 Paperback
ISSN 2753-8117 (online)
ISSN 2753-8109 (print)

Counter-Stereotypes and Attitudes Toward Gender and LGBTQ Equality

Elements in Gender and Politics

DOI: 10.1017/9781009406628
First published online: March 2024

Jae-Hee Jung
University of Houston

Margit Tavits
Washington University in St. Louis

Author for correspondence: Jae-Hee Jung, jjung26@central.uh.edu

Abstract: Insights from social psychology and the gender and politics literature, as well as discussions and campaigns in the policymaking world, suggest that exposure to counter-stereotypes about gender roles might improve people's attitudes toward gender equality and LGBTQ rights. The authors test this expectation by conducting five survey experiments (N=6,916) and a separate, follow-up experiment (N=3,600) in the US context using counter-stereotypical treatments commonly encountered in the real world. They examine both political and nonpolitical attitudes, manipulate stereotypes about both men and women, and provide visual as well as textual stimuli. The treatments undermined stereotypes about the gender roles depicted in the counter-stereotypical exemplars. However, they failed to alter respondents' generic core beliefs about women and men and increase equitable attitudes. The results improve our understanding of how stereotypes contribute to gender and anti-LGBTQ bias.

Keywords: gender stereotypes, gender equality, LGBTQ acceptance, counter-stereotypes, gender roles

ISBNs: 9781009462655 (HB), 9781009406659 (PB), 9781009406628 (OC)
ISSNs: 2753-8117 (online), 2753-8109 (print)

Contents

1 Introduction

Stereotypes about traditional gender roles are often blamed for helping to sustain gender inequalities and attitudes that favor men over women in social, economic, and political domains (Ellemers 2018; Inglehart and Norris 2003; Iversen and Rosenbluth 2010). For example, prominent research shows that gender stereotypes are related to gender gap in science and math achievement (Nosek et al. 2009), predict gender inequality cross-nationally (Glick et al. 2004), affect the assessment of political candidates and vote choice (e.g., Huddy and Terkildsen 1993; Sanbonmatsu 2002), and impede women's career advancement (Eagly and Sczesny 2009; Heilman 2012). These same stereotypes seem to also promote discrimination against sexual and gender minorities (i.e., the LGBTQ population) (Tavits and Pérez 2019; Whitehead 2014). In fact, the 2020 US Supreme Court ruling on discrimination of LGBTQ employees (*Bostock v. Clayton County*) directly attributes LGBTQ discrimination to gender stereotypes.

How can we mitigate these biases and increase gender-equal attitudes and tolerance toward gender and sexual minorities? If inequitable attitudes rest on stereotypes, could undermining these stereotypes and disrupting their application help promote more equitable attitudes about women and the LGBTQ population? Insights from social psychology and the gender and politics literature indeed suggest that counter-stereotypes likely influence attitudes. More specifically, exposure to examples of men and women in counter-stereotypical gender roles (i.e., roles that violate traditional gender norms) may weaken preexisting patriarchal stereotypes, make them less mentally accessible, or incentivize individuals to suppress them. The weakening and/or suppression of gender-role stereotypes could promote not only gender-equitable attitudes, but also attitudes favorable toward sexual and gender minorities given evidence in prior work that prejudice against the LGBTQ community at least partly stems from stereotypes about gender roles. As a result, attitudes are less likely to reflect the pro-male and anti-LGBTQ bias present in traditional gender stereotypes. In other words, we hypothesize that individuals exposed to counter-stereotypes about gender roles are more likely to express gender-equal attitudes and tolerance toward LGBTQ rights.

This intuition underlies many real-life efforts to promote gender counter-stereotypes, in both political and nonpolitical domains. To reduce these inequalities, there are many campaigns at the level of international organizations, national governments, and civil society organizations to reduce stereotypes and promote counter-stereotypes about gender roles. These policy efforts attempt to normalize counter-stereotypes in everyday life. For example, countries have regulatory bodies that monitor advertising content that reinforces gender stereotypes. In 2019, the UK's Advertising Standards Authority introduced a ban on ads featuring "harmful gender stereotypes" on the grounds that they "contribute to inequality in society."[1] At the international level, the United Nations (UN) invests in campaigns to counter gender stereotypes in its member countries. Recently, for instance, there was a collaboration between UN Women, UN Population Fund, Biasless (a Ukrainian civil society organization), and the European Union to fight gender stereotypes in Tiktok in Ukraine. Furthermore, there are movements to counter stereotypes in everyday products such as children's clothing.[2] There are also numerous online platforms that collate ads and campaigns that subvert gender stereotypes.[3] All in all, these efforts take place with the expectation that exposure to counter-stereotypes can be helpful for reducing inequitable attitudes.

Yet this intuition has not been directly tested in academic work. For sure, the intuition clearly underlies scholarly arguments about the benefits of gender quotas and female role models. For example, gender quotas are expected to decrease gender inequalities because women who become political or corporate (or other type of) leaders undermine stereotypes about what women can achieve (Beaman et al. 2012; Krook 2010; O'Brien and Rickne 2016). Increasing the number of female role models in politics or other male-dominant roles is similarly seen as a way to break old stereotypes about women's limited competence in these domains (Barnes and Burchard 2013; Beaman et al. 2009; Matland 1994). More generally, this intuition is also in line with implications stemming from findings about the role of contact in prejudice reduction (Pettigrew and Tropp 2006), according to which diverse environments and increased interaction with out-group members can undermine biased representations and attitudes. While these studies provide support for the general intuition, they are not designed to isolate the effect of counter-stereotypes.

The effects of gender counter-stereotypes on attitudes have received limited attention in social psychology as well. Prior work in this field has examined counter-stereotypes, but has focused more on racial bias than gender, and not at all on LGBTQ issues. Both types of biases continue to be significant problems, both in the US and globally, with anti-LGBTQ bias potentially worsening in recent years: for example, data collected by the Public Religion Research Institute (PRRI) show that the share of Americans who believe that there are only two genders has increased from 59 percent in 2021 to 65 percent in 2023.[4] The persistence of gender inequality (Damann et al. 2023) and the worsening anti-LGBTQ bias clearly highlight the need to better understand attitudes in these domains.

In addition to the lack of attention to gender and LGBTQ attitudes, prior work has primarily been conducted in the lab rather than among mass publics, and has not considered politically relevant stereotypes and outcomes. Furthermore, previous studies focus on whether counter-stereotypes reduce prejudice in implicit attitudes (e.g., Blair et al. 2001; Dasgupta and Greenwald 2001; Lai et al. 2014), which are automatic, visceral responses to an attitude object that can be measured with tools such as the Implicit Association Test (IAT). Previous studies have paid less attention to verbally expressed explicit attitudes, which are cognitive, controlled evaluations that can be measured through survey questions. Yet, from societal perspective, explicit attitudes are equally relevant for understanding prejudice and discrimination (see Ditonto et al. 2013; Mo 2015). In fact, both gender and LGBTQ intolerance is often expressed explicitly, verbally, and behaviorally, including by extremist political forces that are gaining ground in many societies today. Some suggest that, in this domain, explicit attitudes may be more relevant than implicit ones for predicting behavior (Oswald et al. 2013).

We advance prior work by addressing these limitations. We isolate the effect of exposure to counter-stereotypical gender roles; explore the domains of gender and LGBTQ equality; study explicit, socially and politically relevant attitudes; include political as well as nonpolitical counter-stereotypes; and take the study outside of the lab by employing a series of mass surveys. As a further advancement, we explore the effects of counter-stereotypical treatments that can be easily adopted and encountered in the real world (e.g., in textbooks, media, or any other written or visual materials) in order to provide practical insights to policymakers. This also has the benefit of increasing the external validity of our experimental setting.

We test our expectations through a series of five survey experiments (N=6,916) in the US context using counter-stereotypical treatments commonly encountered in the real world. The first three studies differ in the type of counter-stereotypical treatment used. Study 1 uses a description of God and randomizes whether God is referred to with a male (stereotypical) or female (counter-stereotypical) pronoun. Studies 2 and 3 administer treatments that have visual stimuli in addition to textual stimuli and extend Study 1 in other ways. Study 2 uses the presidency as a stereotypically male position, and randomizes exposure to information and a picture of male (stereotypical) or female (counter-stereotypical) presidents. Study 3 reverses the gender stereotype and uses housekeeper as a stereotypically female position. It randomizes exposure to information and a picture of a female (stereotypical) or male (counter-stereotypical) housekeeper. To indicate that there is social acceptance of the counter-stereotype, which is known to be important for moving implicit attitudes (Finnegan et al. 2015) and underlies many real-life counter-stereotype campaigns, the vignettes use descriptions of God, president, and housekeeper from authoritative sources with reference to the source. Study 4 is a placebo test. It uses a gender-neutral profession – a singer – and does not contain (counter-) stereotypical information. We conducted this study because if we find counter-stereotypes influencing attitudes as expected, a placebo study manipulating the gender association of a role where there is no gender stereotype should yield null results. Study 5 combines the treatments used in Studies 1–3 and provides stronger treatments that intensify the amount of counter-stereotypical information received. Across all studies, posttreatment, respondents answered questions on gender equality and issues of homosexuality and transgender people.

We find consistently null results. We do not find evidence that exposure to counter-stereotypical information about gender roles affects attitudes toward gender equality in either social or political domains and tolerance toward the LGBTQ population. This null finding holds across all studies, regardless of whether the counter-stereotype (a) relates to political (Study 2) or nonpolitical (Studies 1 and 3) domain, (b) refers to women (Studies 1 and 2) or men (Study 3), (c) relies on only textual (Study 1) or textual and visual (Studies 2 and 3) stimulus, or (d) includes all those features (Study 5). The null effects are robust to a host of additional analyses. We also demonstrate that they cannot be explained by lack of statistical power. As expected, the placebo study (Study 4), that is, simply making one of the genders salient, without counter-stereotypical stimulus, also has no effect on gender-equitable and LGBTQ attitudes.

To understand the null results, we show that they are not due to subgroup heterogeneity or ceiling effects. We also demonstrate that they cannot be explained by failure to uptake the treatment. We instead explore the possibility that the loosening of stereotypes caused by the counter-stereotypical exemplars did not generalize to overall gender- and LGBTQ-related attitudes. To test this possibility, we ran a separate follow-up experiment (N=3,600). We find that the treatments undermined stereotypes about the gender roles depicted in the counter-stereotypical exemplars. However, they did not alter respondents' generic core beliefs about women and men and hence did not increase equitable attitudes. In other words, while the counter-stereotypical information successfully undermined stereotypes about the specific roles presented in the treatments, they left respondents' generic core beliefs about women and men unaltered, which most likely accounts for the null effects on our attitudinal outcomes of interest.

These null results are important given the strong theoretical backing for the original expectation as well as the real-life relevance of the treatments that we used. The results indicate that while gender-role counter-stereotypes are assumed to be helpful in reducing gender and LGBTQ bias, they do not necessarily achieve that. In other words, exposure to counter-stereotypes that is commonly used in real-life campaigns is not sufficient to increase equitable attitudes. The results provide insights on the kinds of interventions that may be required to change gender and LGBTQ attitudes. Passive exposure to specific counter-stereotypical examples, no matter how realistic or strong, does not seem enough to alter attitudes (see also Tavits et al. 2024). Instead, an important implication of our work is that one might need to combine strong, realistic counter-stereotypes (as we did in our experiments) with chronic, active, and experiential exposure to produce effects – something that future studies and policymakers should focus on. This Element speaks to the wide array of efforts taking place in political and nonpolitical sectors to counter public-facing messages that reinforce gender stereotypes. Our findings speak to political and nonpolitical policy communities that are working to introduce and reinforce counter-stereotypes in order to improve equitability.

These implications are of interest to scholars as well. We speak to political scientists who study topics of gender bias and LGBTQ bias by isolating the effect of counter-stereotypes about gender roles, which has not been directly investigated in prior work. Previous studies have examined the effects of counter-stereotypes, but they typically either study *trait* counter-stereotypes (e.g., Bauer 2020; Bernhard 2021), such as portraying women as aggressive and men as caring, or study gender-role counter-stereotypes in conjunction with trait counter-stereotypes (e.g., Bauer 2017). Moreover, while these studies are specifically interested in counter-stereotypes about political candidates and examine their effects on people's assessments of those candidates, our work goes beyond the electoral context and examines attitudes on issues and policies more generally. We also contribute to social psychology by examining the effect of gender counter-stereotypes on explicit attitudes. This contrasts with previous work that has mainly focused on stereotypes about race and implicit attitudes in that issue area.

The rest of the Element is structured as follows. The second section develops the theory and expectation. We discuss that exposure to counter-stereotypes can weaken preexisting associations that shape people's attitudes and that counterstereotypes can make people suppress such associations, thereby leading to more gender-equal attitudes and liberalized views toward the LGBTQ community. In terms of encouraging gender-equal attitudes, exposure to examples of men and women in counter-stereotypical gender roles (i.e., roles that violate traditional gender norms) may weaken preexisting patriarchal stereotypes, make them less mentally accessible, or incentivize individuals to suppress them. As a result, attitudes are less likely to be biased along gender lines, with individuals more accepting of women and men in a variety of social roles. Weakening and suppressing stereotypes about gender roles may affect attitudes toward LGBTQ equality as well. Since previous work shows that prejudice against the LGBTQ community is also at least partly rooted in perceptions that these individuals violate traditional gender roles, when stereotypes about what constitute gender roles get redefined to be more inclusive and less rigid, it is possible that what was considered a violation is no longer perceived as such. This, in turn, could lead to individuals expressing more liberalized attitudes about nontraditional gender identities and sexual orientations. We explain that this argument is consistent with insights from the gender and politics literature and the social psychology literature on stereotypes. In developing the theory, we draw connections between studies of gender; sexual and gender minorities; and public opinion in political science as well as psychology.

The third section presents the design principles of the five main experiments we conducted. The data include both probability-based and non-probability-based samples of the adult population in the US. Our experiments use (counter-) stereotypical depictions of God, presidents, and housekeepers. This allows us to study both political and nonpolitical roles with clear gender associations, which we undermine through counter-stereotypical information. The vignettes use pictures and texts that reinforce counter-stereotypical definitions of the figure of interest (e.g., presidents as women), along with reference to an authoritative source that signals the normality of such associations. We are interested in the effects of normalized, embedded counter-stereotypes in everyday life. While these have received little attention in prior work on counter-stereotypes, they are inspired by the literature on prejudice reduction. This literature sees social norms, that we argue can be reflected in normalized, everyday (as opposed to unusual or sensational) counter-stereotypes, as one potential way to decrease prejudicial attitudes (Tankard and Paluck 2017; see also Jung and Tavits 2021a). With this in mind, we explore the effects of counter-stereotypical treatments that can be easily adopted and encountered in the real world (e.g., in textbooks, media, or any other written or visual materials). In this section, we also discuss the design of a placebo experiment that uses a gender-neutral role – singer. Additionally, we show the results of a separate test of gender associations (N=300) that demonstrate the appropriateness of using God, presidents, house-keepers, and singers as the subjects of our experimental vignettes. We test for the effects of all these vignettes on expressed attitudes about gender and LGBTQ equality, in both social and political domains.

In the fourth section, we present the results of the five experiments. Three of those experiments use counter-stereotypical versus stereotypical depictions of God, presidents, and housekeepers. One of those experiments is a placebo study that uses the role of a singer, which does not have any gender associations. Again, the rationale for this study was that we should observe null results when manipulating the gender association of a role that does not have either feminine or masculine stereotypes. The last experiment uses the same vignettes about God, presidents, and housekeepers used in the first three experiments, but we strengthen the treatment by presenting respondents with (counter-)stereotypical information on all of those roles, not just one of them. Analyses of these experiments consistently yield null results. Series of additional analyses demonstrate the robustness of these null findings.

In the fifth section, we explore what explains the null results. We start by showing that these null effects are not because of ceiling effects or subgroup effects. We discuss theoretically that the null results are unlikely to be because respondents dismiss counter-stereotypical information as an anomaly or because respondents see counter-stereotypical information as a signal that sufficient equality has been achieved. Rather, through a separate additional experiment (N=3,600), we find that while the counter-stereotypical manipulation we used loosened the gender associations of the specific role depicted in the counter-stereotypical example, the effect did not generalize outside of the specific example. In other words, we find that the counter-stereotype treatments indeed increase counter-stereotypical gender associations of the role of interest, suggesting that the manipulation worked as intended. However, respondents' generic beliefs about women and men remained unaffected, as measured by the extent to which respondents think a set of particular adjectives describe men and women. We conclude that this is why we do not find evidence that counter-stereotype treatments increase overall equitable attitudes about gender and the LGBTQ population. Note that this conclusion is similar to findings in the prejudice reduction literature, which has demonstrated that institutional and/or informational interventions are able to effectively alter perceptions of social norms, but that this does not necessarily translate into attitude change (see Jung and Tavits 2021a; Tankard and Paluck 2017; Thompson 2022).

The sixth section concludes. This final section discusses the implications of our findings for scholars and policymakers. The results indicate that while gender counter-stereotypes are assumed to be helpful in reducing gender and LGBTQ bias, they do not necessarily achieve that. The results provide the insight that the kinds of interventions that may be required to change gender and LGBTQ attitudes are likely to be of the sort that is active, chronic, and experiential. Our research shows that there is much connection between the literatures on gender and the LGBTQ community, as well as the political science and psychology literatures on stereotypes, that need to be further explored. We discuss how our findings speak to the wide array of efforts taking place in political and nonpolitical sectors of society to counter public-facing messages that reinforce gender stereotypes. Moreover, we discuss how increased women and LGBTQ representation in politics in recent years fits into the normalization of counter-stereotypes.

2 Theory: Counter-stereotypes and Attitudes

Social psychologists define stereotypes as generic cognitive beliefs about a social group (Fiske 1998; Zuo et al. 2019). They are collections of traits and attributes that are viewed as typically or strongly associated with that group (Blair et al. 2001). For example, one's stereotype of the elderly or women may include perceptions about typical physical characteristics (e.g., the elderly are ailing; women are fragile), personality traits (e.g., the elderly are dependent; women are caring), and social roles (e.g., the elderly are retired; women are nurses or secretaries). In short, stereotypes reflect what is normal and expected about a given social group.

Stereotypes serve a useful purpose of allowing individuals to categorize and simplify the world and predict the behavior of others (Ellemers 2018; Fiske and Taylor 2013). However, they can also lead to faulty and biased judgment because generalizations ignore the specific qualities of an individual. Relying on stereotypes can therefore contribute to prejudiced attitudes and behavior toward members of a given group (Fiske 1998). Furthermore, because they concern generic core beliefs about a group and refer to associations that are typical and strong, stereotypes are likely to be highly mentally accessible (Bodenhausen et al. 2009) and people are likely to consider them when forming and expressing attitudes about that group (Blair et al. 2001; Peffley et al. 1997).

This suggests that in order to decrease stereotype biases, one needs to weaken the stereotype or decrease its accessibility (Blair et al. 2001; Finnegan et al. 2015). Psychological research suggests that this could be achieved by exposure to counter-stereotypes, which are attributes and traits that are *inconsistent with* or *contrary to* the ones typically associated with that group (Leicht et al. 2017; Liu and Zuo 2006; Zuo et al. 2019). For example, in the domain of racial stereotypes, studies have used scenarios where a White man commits an assault and a Black man rescues the victim as counter-stereotypical exemplars (Lai et al. 2014).

Since counter-stereotypes refer to associations that are atypical, abnormal, or unexpected, information about them is not highly mentally accessible. For example, people do not usually expect the elderly to be athletic or women to be aggressive. Unlike stereotypes, counter-stereotypes therefore do not regularly influence judgment about a group (Blair et al. 2001). However, exposing individuals to counter-stereotypical information brings these atypical associations to the fore, forcing the individual to consider them. This mental accessibility of the new associations could weaken the effect of stereotypes on attitudes by (a) weakening these stereotypes because of the wider range of associations that now apply to the group (Finnegan et al. 2015; Operario and Fiske 2004), and/or (b) decreasing the use of these stereotypes because individuals may rely entirely on the new associations instead of the existing stereotypes when expressing attitudes about members of the group (Finnegan et al. 2015). That is, counter-stereotypical information about a group leads individuals to update their cognitive representations of that group. The specific content of earlier stereotypes is no longer predominant and effective in affecting attitudes because individuals are triggered to "think outside the box" about possibilities beyond the ones included in stereotypes. Since stereotypes are weakened or overrun by other associations, individuals are likely to express less biased attitudes toward members of the group than they would if they only relied on stereotypes. Prior work has indeed shown, for example, that individuals exposed to positive exemplars of Blacks and negative exemplars of Whites (i.e., counter-stereotypical information about each group) express less negative attitudes toward Blacks (Dasgupta and Greenwald 2001; see also Lai et al. 2014).

These arguments have been used to explain the effect of counter-stereotypical exemplars on *implicit* bias in various domains. However, because stereotypes also affect explicit attitudes, these same mechanisms can explain why counter-stereotypes might also reduce conscious verbal or behavioral expressions of bias (see Gawronski and Bodenhausen 2006; Carruthers 2018; in political science, see Dolan 2010; Huddy and Terkildsen 1993; Hurwitz and Peffley 1997; Mo 2015; Sanbonmatsu 2002). Furthermore, counter-stereotypes may reduce explicit bias by increasing individuals' motivation to suppress using stereotypes. A long line of research suggests that prejudice reduction requires perceivers to be aware of their biases and to be motivated to not rely on them (e.g., Allport 1954; Fiske 1998). Being exposed to counter-stereotypes about a social group may reveal to individuals their reliance on stereotypes and motivate them to consciously avoid stereotyping when expressing their attitudes (Peffley et al. 1997). In short, we expect that exposure to counter-stereotypical information about a specific social group decreases bias in attitudes toward members of that group.

2.1 Application to the Domain of Gender and LGBTQ Equality

We now apply these arguments to explain how counter-stereotypes about gender roles can affect attitudes about the gender and LGBTQ domains. As is the case with other social groups, stereotypes about gender are generic beliefs about what women and men are like. They rely on differences in traditional gender roles (Ellemers 2018; Koenig and Eagly 2014) and, congruent with those social roles, men are characterized as more agentic (i.e., taking charge and being in control) while women are characterized as more communal (i.e., oriented toward others, caring, nurturing) (Bauer 2015; Eagly and Karau 2002). This corresponds with expecting to see men in powerful, public, and leadership roles and women in domestic, caretaker, and service roles (Holman et al. 2016; see also Dolan 2014; Huddy and Terkildsen 1993; Koch 2000; Sanbonmatsu 2002).

As argued previously, because stereotypes concern generic core beliefs about a group and refer to typical and strong associations, they are likely to be highly mentally accessible and people are likely to consider them when forming and expressing attitudes about that group (Blair et al. 2001; Peffley et al. 1997). This is equally true for stereotypes about gender roles. Ditonto et al. (2014) show, for example, that gender stereotypes lead people to look for different kinds of information about female political candidates compared to male candidates. Schneider et al. (2022) show that people punish agentic female candidates for violating expected gender roles. Stereotypes may be influential enough such that campaign attacks by rivals on female candidates' stereotypically feminine strengths hurt people's evaluations of and votes for those female candidates (Cassese and Holman 2018). Many other studies show that such stereotypes feed gender-unequal attitudes and outcomes in politics and elsewhere (e.g., Dolan 2014; Finnegan et al. 2015; Glick et al. 2004; Huddy and Terkildsen 1993; Koch 2000; Matland 1994; Sanbonmatsu 2002). These attitudes (a) exhibit pro-male bias in socio-economic and political life and, (b) view gender inequalities as natural and acceptable, while efforts to rectify the imbalances as unnecessary. In short, stereotypes about traditional gender roles are likely to sustain unequal attitudes about women and men.[5] Sexist and gendered beliefs in turn affect evaluations of politicians (Costa 2021; Ditonto 2019) and voting behavior for both women and men (Cassese and Barnes 2019; Deckman and Cassese 2021; Ditonto 2019).

Exposure to counter-stereotypes about gender roles might be able to counteract these detrimental effects. As explained previously, counter-stereotypes provide new and alternative associations about a group. For example, they

---

[5] Some previous research shows that gender stereotypes are not central to the disadvantages that female political candidates experience in terms of evaluation and the vote (Brooks 2011; 2013; Dolan 2014), or that stereotypes hurt female candidates only when they are activated during the campaign (Bauer 2015). Furthermore, gender stereotypes interact with party stereotypes such that in the American context, female Republican politicians are not as disadvantaged as female Democratic politicians (Holman, Merolla, and Zechmeister 2011; 2016). However, we focus on general gender attitudes and not specifically electoral contexts, and there are many studies discussed in this section that show the importance of stereotypes.

may associate women with being strong and men with being weak, or women as being powerful and men as caring. Mental accessibility of the new associations likely weakens the effect of stereotypes on attitudes by (a) weakening stereotypes because of the wider range of associations that now apply to the group (Finnegan et al. 2015; Operario and Fiske 2004), and/or (b) decreasing the use of stereotypes because individuals may start relying entirely on the new associations when expressing attitudes about members of the group (Finnegan et al. 2015). In short, we expect that while stereotypes motivate individuals to see gender roles as distinct and unequal, counter-stereotypes blur those distinctions and inequalities. Therefore, individuals exposed to counter-stereotypes about gender roles are more likely to express gender-equal attitudes. This serves as our first hypothesis.

Weakening and suppressing stereotypes about gender roles may affect attitudes toward LGBTQ equality as well. Prior work argues that prejudice against the LGBTQ community is rooted in perceptions that they violate traditional gender roles (e.g., Blashill and Powlishta 2009; Lehavot and Lambert 2007; Tavits and Pérez 2019; Whitehead 2014), which include expectations about sexual behavior, masculinity, and femininity. Stereotypes about homosexuality are tightly linked to violations of gender roles, where homosexuals are considered similar to heterosexuals of the opposite sex (Kite and Deaux 1987; Madon 1997). In the transgender domain, those who perceive greater difference between men and women and find conforming to gender norms personally important are less supportive of transgender identity (Becker and Jones 2021). Since prejudice against the LGBTQ community is at least partly rooted in perceptions that these individuals violate traditional gender roles (Becker and Jones 2021; Blashill and Powlishta 2009; Kite and Deaux 1987; Lehavot and Lambert 2007; Madon 1997; Pérez and Tavits 2022; Tavits and Pérez 2019; Whitehead 2014), when stereotypes about what constitute gender roles get redefined to be more inclusive and less rigid, it is possible that what was considered a violation is no longer perceived as such. This suggests that, as a result of exposure to gender counter-stereotypes, traditional stereotypes are weakened and/or suppressed, making individuals express more liberalized attitudes about nontraditional gender identities and sexual orientations. Therefore, we also hypothesize that exposure to counter-stereotypes about gender roles increases equitability and tolerance toward LGBTQ rights. Our goal here is to examine gender counter-stereotypes and their percolating effects on attitudes about the LGBTQ. Our intention is similar to previous work that examines spillover and transfer effects (e.g., Pettigrew 2009; Simonovits et al. 2018). Therefore, while the relationship between beliefs about gender roles and attitudes about the LGBTQ is not as direct as that between beliefs about gender roles and attitudes about gender equality, we posit the same theoretical mechanism for LGBTQ attitudes: exposure to counter-stereotypical gender roles could weaken stereotypes and/or decrease reliance on those stereotypes, thereby leading to more supportive attitudes about sexual and gender minorities.

To clarify, we study attitudes about lesbians, gays, and bisexuals (LGB) as well as transgender people because they are all marginalized communities that are affected by views about traditional gender roles. This is shown in the literature that we just reviewed, and acknowledged in real-life discussions of LGBTQ discrimination. For example, as mentioned in the first section, the 2020 US Supreme Court ruling (*Bostock v. Clayton County*) attributed discrimination of LGBTQ employees to gender stereotypes. Justice Neil Gorsuch wrote, "An employer who fired an individual for being homosexual or transgender fires that person for traits or actions it would not have questioned in members of a different sex."[6] Moreover, research shows that because the topic of transgender rights is significantly more nascent, people tend to transfer their experiences with and attitudes about the LGB to their views on transgender rights (Flores 2015). In short, the two domains are highly related (see also Norton and Herek 2013). That said, the LGBTQ population is diverse, and attitudes about the rights of the different subgroups can vary. For example, earlier studies showed that attitudes about the transgender population tended to be more negative (Lewis et al. 2017).[7] Recent data collected by the Public Religion Research Institute (PRRI) however show that the gap may not be as large: in 2023, about 48 percent of Americans were somewhat or very comfortable with learning that a friend is in a relationship with someone of the same gender, and 41 percent feel that way when learning that a friend is transgender.[8]

Since our focus is on the effects of counter-stereotypes about gender roles, we do not theorize about counter-stereotypes that are specifically about LGBTQ individuals, such as depictions of gay men as masculine and lesbian people as feminine. That is an avenue for future research. And we acknowledge that prejudice against LGBTQ individuals is not only rooted in perceptions that these individuals violate traditional gender roles. Other sources of prejudice toward gay men and lesbian women and their rights include violations of sexual orientation (Lehavot and Lambert 2007) and beliefs about whether sexual orientation is genetic or not (Haider-Markel and Joslyn 2005, 2008; Joslyn and Haider-Markel 2016). When it comes to attitudes about transgender people

---

[6] https://www.nbcnews.com/politics/supreme-court/supreme-court-rules-existing-civil-rights-law-protects-gay-lesbian-n1231018#

[7] In the empirical analyses, we examine attitudes toward LGB and transgender people separately as well as together.

[8] https://www.prri.org/research/the-politics-of-gender-pronouns-and-public-education/

and their rights, predictors include ignorance or lack of interpersonal contact (Flores 2015), empathy emanating from personal experiences with gender discrimination (Becker and Jones 2021), and cognitive need for closure (Jones et al. 2018).

But how do our expectations relate to previous studies in social psychology on the effects of counter-stereotypes? As mentioned previously, most prior work focuses on understanding implicit attitudes. That is especially the case in the gender domain. Blair et al. (2001) examine the effect of counter-stereotypical mental imagery (i.e., having participants imagine a strong woman and her qualities and features). Finnegan et al. (2015) present participants with information of hypothetical men and women in counter-stereotypical job environments (e.g., picture of Rebecca, a bricklayer). Dasgupta and Asgari (2004) investigate the effects of counter-stereotypic women leaders (e.g., biographical information about famous female leaders). All these studies find stereotype-reducing effects as measured through the Implicit Association Test.

But some studies have examined explicit attitudes, and they are mainly in the race domain. Those studies in social psychology report inconsistent or weak effects of counter-stereotypes on explicit attitudes. Dasgupta and Greenwald (2001) do not find that exemplars of admired Black and disliked White individuals (e.g., Denzel Washington and Jeffrey Dahmer, respectively) reduce White-biased prejudice in explicit attitudes like feeling thermometers. Joy-Gaba and Nosek (2010) do a replication of Dasgupta and Greenwald's work and again find that such exemplars do not improve explicit attitudes. Lai et al. (2014), in their survey of seventeen kinds of interventions, find that strategies using counter-stereotypical exemplars do not reliably reduce explicit bias. One of the different interventions they use that fall under counter-stereotypical exemplar usage is again presentation of famous Black people (e.g., Bill Cosby) and infamous White people (e.g., Charles Manson). Lai et al. (2016) find similar results in their subsequent article that focuses on the longevity of effects. Nonetheless, we explore the effect of counter-stereotypes on explicit attitudes in the gender domain for a couple of reasons. First, those studies cover explicit attitudes in passing, as their primary focus is to understand implicit attitudes – they are not purposefully designed to test explicit attitudes, and do not offer a theoretical explanation of their findings. For example, the studies typically say something along the following lines, at most, to justify inclusion of explicit attitudes in their work: "The focus of the research contest is on reducing implicit preferences. However, it is of theoretical and practical interest to also understand what interventions are effective at changing explicit preferences" (Lai et al. 2014, 11). Second, extant studies on explicit attitudes generally focus on racial attitudes rather than gender. Yet the gender domain might be more malleable than the race domain because while racial groups can avoid contact with each other, men and women are necessarily tied to each other due to kinship relations (see Glick and Fiske 1997). Therefore, a direct and focused investigation of explicit attitudes in the gender domain is needed. Furthermore, we go a step further and examine the effects of gender counter-stereotypes on attitudes about the LGBTQ population.

While we derive our expectations primarily from the psychology literature, they are also in line with various theories in the gender literature. For example, gender schema theory (Bem 1981) and social role theory (Koenig and Eagly 2014) suggest that (a) gender stereotypical environment fosters stereotype-congruent behavior and attitudes, which implies that (b) interventions involving exposure to gender counter-stereotypes can enhance equitable aspirations (Costa and Wallace 2021; Olsson and Martiny 2018). Moreover, studies in political science find that counter-stereotypical depictions of female political candidates reduce stereotyping and improve attitudes about the candidates. Counter-stereotypical information increase counter-stereotypical trait ratings and likeability and improve evaluations of leadership qualities and issue competences held by the candidate (Bauer 2017, 2020; Schneider 2014). They can even increase favorable attitudes toward real-life, rather than hypothetical, female politicians (Bernhard 2021). These studies do not examine the effect of counter-stereotypes about gender roles per se, because they are interested in the effects of trait counter-stereotype or counter-stereotypes more generally. They are also focused strictly on electoral contexts, unlike ours, which explores the effects of normalized counter-stereotypical information in everyday life on general (rather than electoral) attitudes. Nonetheless, our theoretical expectations are in line with research on counter-stereotypes in gender and politics.

Our expectations are also highly intuitive and underlie real-world policy interventions to increase gender equality through exposure to counter-stereotypical gender roles – from initiatives to hire more male teachers to implementation of various gender quotas (Barnes and Burchard 2013; Matland 1994; Olsson and Martiny 2018). In short, there are strong theoretical reasons to expect that exposure to gender counter-stereotypes enhances equitable attitudes, and there are important practical reasons to explore whether this is the case, not only in the area of attitudes about men versus women, but also in the area of attitudes about sexual and gender minorities. We begin that exploration in the next section.

3 Experimental Research Design

In this section, we present the design principles of the five main experiments that we conducted to test our hypotheses. The data include both probability-based and non-probability-based samples of the US adult population. The experiments are embedded in surveys and use a between-subjects design. In three of those experiments (Studies 1–3), one group is presented with an example of men (women) in a stereotypical role and the other group with an example of women (men) in a counter-stereotypical role.[9] Study 5 has the same design, but each group of respondents is presented with three (counter-)stereotypical vignettes, instead of one. Burgess and Borgida (1999) explain that gender stereotypes have two components: descriptive (how women/men are) and prescriptive (how women/men should be). In our treatments, we do not distinguish the two but try to undermine both by presenting counter-stereotypical information about how women/men are and can be. Study 4 is a placebo experiment that uses examples of men and women in a role that is neither stereotypical nor counter-stereotypical. Since our theoretical expectation is that counter-stereotypical treatments will move attitudes about gender equality and LGBTQ rights, in addition to Studies 1–3, we also wanted to do an experiment to test that in the absence of counter-stereotypes, we do not observe such movement in attitudes. That is the rationale for Study 4. Study 5 was conducted after Studies 1–4 were completed. It tests for the effect of counter-stereotypical gender roles by combining the vignettes used in Studies 1–3 and thus intensifies the treatment.

In order to best assess the effects of exposure to counter-stereotypes, our goal was to design strong and realistic interventions. To achieve this, we did the following. First, we use treatments that can be encountered in the real world and easily implemented by policymakers. All of our treatments are of the kind that can be embedded in books, advertisements, print or digital media, and other such materials. Second, because prior research on counter-stereotypes calls for more complex stimuli than simple category labels (Finnegan et al. 2015), our manipulations use descriptions, not labels (in all five studies), and visual in addition to textual stimuli (in four of the five studies). Third, since social acceptance of the counter-stereotype potentially enhances its effect (Finnegan et al. 2015)[10] and counter-stereotype campaigns in the real world present information matter-of-factly, our interventions signal acceptance and normality by using descriptions from authoritative sources with reference to the source. Fourth, we used a combination of post-test and pre-tests to verify that the roles we chose for Studies 1, 2, 3, and 5 are perceived strongly (counter-)stereotypical and reinforced the treatments with

---

[9] A within-subjects design where respondents receive both conditions does not work because once we present counter-stereotypical (stereotypical) information, that information cannot be erased before we subsequently present stereotypical (counter-stereotypical) information.

[10] Along the same lines, studies on prejudice reduction have also sought to better understand how social norms could be used to change attitudes (see Jung and Tavits 2021a; Pérez and Tavits 2019; 2022; Tanckard and Paluck 2017).

comprehension questions. We also used a pre-test to pick a role for Study 4 that does not have gender associations. While our treatments are one-shot, our design is in line with one-shot lab experimental treatments conducted in prior psychological work. We describe the details of the design of each study in turn.

3.1 Study 1

We conducted Study 1 in August 2017 as part of The American Panel Survey (TAPS). TAPS is an online monthly panel survey of a nationally representative sample of about 2,000 U.S. adults using address-based probability sampling. The panel started in December 2011 and was fielded by GfK. The sample size for Study 1 is 2,111, i.e., about 1,000 respondents in each experimental arm. TAPS collects sociodemographic information on its panelists, of which we use gender, age, education, household income, race, political ideology, and region.

Study 1 examines the influence of counter-stereotypical information in the context of religion. Our study started with a manipulation, where respondents were randomized to read a text describing God using either male or female pronouns. Since God is typically thought of as male,[11] the female-God vignette is the counter-stereotype treatment. Here we are manipulating the prevailing male gender association of God. That said, the use of female pronouns to describe God is not unheard of. Many branches of Christianity refer to God using female pronouns,[12] and many people acknowledge that God is neither a man nor a woman although masculine pronouns and images are typically used to refer to and describe God.[13] In fact, God is typically thought to have feminine features as well (e.g., compassion). To make sure that respondents perceived the description of God as credible and widely accepted, the text provided a theological definition of God from *The Oxford Companion to Philosophy*. After reading the text, respondents were asked a factual question about what they read. The question and response options reinforced the treatment by using the same pronoun as the text. Answers to the question can also be used as an attention check, with 90 percent of respondents choosing the correct answer. The correct answer was "All of the above," meaning that the other answer options were technically correct as well. Therefore, the 90 percent passage rate is a conservative estimate of those who were attentive to the survey.

---

[11] For existing survey evidence of this, see, for example, https://www.statista.com/statistics/297237/united-states-god-gender-male-female/.

[12] https://theconversation.com/what-the-early-church-thought-about-gods-gender-100077

[13] https://www.bbc.com/news/magazine-32960507

After treatment, we asked respondents about their views on gender equality and gender and sexual minorities. Specifically, we inquired respondents, on a five-point scale, how much they agree or disagree with the following statements: "wives do not have to do more housework than husbands do" (item name: *Housework*); "when jobs are scarce, men have more right to a job than women" (*Jobs*); "political parties should do more to encourage qualified women to run for political office" (*Parties*); "on the whole, men make better political leaders than women do" (*Leaders*); "I do not want immigrant/foreign workers as neighbors" (*Neighbor*); and "homosexual couples should be able to marry one another" (*Gay*). The first four are about gender equality. The fifth statement on foreigners is a placebo outcome, one that does not directly measure gender attitudes. This statement captures prejudice about immigrants/foreigners, not women and gender and sexual minorities. Even if people's attitudes about gender and race often correlate (see, e.g., Schaffner 2022b), we do not expect attitudes in the xenophobia domain to be causally affected by gender counter-stereotypes. The sixth statement (*Gay*) is about LGBTQ equality.[14] These six questions are modeled after high-profile surveys such as the World Values Survey and the General Social Survey. Specifically, the question wording for *Leaders* is taken verbatim from the World Values Survey. The wording for *Jobs* closely mirrors that in the World Values Survey: "When jobs are scarce, men should have more right to a job than women." The wording for *Parties* was inspired by the following question in the General Social Survey: "Because of past discrimination, employers should make special efforts to hire and promote qualified women." The wording for *Housework* is ours and modeled after the other questions as an easy-to-understand statement. The wording for *Neighbor* is an adaptation of the following question in the World Values Survey: "Could you please mention any that you would not like to have as neighbors?" One of the options is "immigrants/foreign workers." The question wording for *Gay* is taken verbatim from the General Social Survey. Overall, we sought to have a mix of question wordings, some of which are positive and some of which are negative, as well as some items to which agreement indicates a response in the equitable direction and some items to which agreement indicates response in the inequitable direction, which helps guard against straight-lining by respondents.

All in all, we chose these questions because they cover the domains of gender and LGBTQ equality and are the outcomes that we expect to be influenced by the female-God treatment, that is, information that gender roles can be fluid. Exposure to information about God being presented in female terms could

---

[14] Study 1 was an exploratory study, so we included only one item about gay marriage to measure attitudes about the LGBTQ. As will be explained, however, Studies 2 and onwards included more questions in the LGBTQ domain, specifically about transgender rights.

weaken or help respondents suppress stereotypical associations, leading them to express more equitable views about the division of household labor and relative economic and political authority between genders. Such weaker binary views about gender roles could also lead respondents to be more supportive of marriage between two men or two women. Moreover, we wanted our questions to measure more descriptive attitudes rather than prescriptive attitudes because our experimental treatments present descriptive, matter-of-fact information on counter-stereotypical role associations. That is why the wordings for *Housework, Jobs,* and *Leaders* are not explicit statements about how gender roles *should* be. At the same time, it is not feasible to measure attitudes in all domains without measuring what ought to be done, which is why the question wordings for *Parties* and *Gay* are phrased in terms of "should." Therefore, our outcome questions get at both descriptive and prescriptive attitudes (Burgess and Borgida 1999) about women and sexual and gender minorities. They can also be considered similar to the modern sexism scale, which Schaffner (2022a) describes as capturing "the extent to which individuals deny the existence of sex-based discrimination, are antagonistic toward demands for equality, and are resentful toward special favors for women" (366).[15]

In what follows, we show the treatments and the outcome questions.

Female God Treatment
Here is a description of how philosophical theologians define God. Please read this information carefully and answer the question at the bottom to continue with the survey.

God has the property of being the greatest conceivable being. She has infinite knowledge and unlimited power. She is present everywhere. She embodies perfect goodness, divine simplicity, and eternal existence. She is creator and sustainer of any universe there may be.

Source: *The Oxford Companion to Philosophy* (Honderich 2005)

According to the description, which attribute does God possess?
- She has infinite knowledge.
- She has perfect goodness.
- She has unlimited power.
- All of the above.

---

[15] Some might point out that the outcome questions we use measure more fundamental attitudes than those reflected in vote choice or candidate preference. While that is true, accessibility of (counter-) stereotypical considerations still shapes attitudes of the sort we are interested in (Zaller 1992), and our exploration of attitudes outside of the election context is precisely one of the contributions we are making to the literature. The counter-stereotypes in our experiments are expected to increase the salience of counter-stereotypes among respondents who receive that information, which in turn may result in expression of attitudes that are more equitable in direction.

Male God Treatment

Here is a description of how philosophical theologians define God. Please read this information carefully and answer the question at the bottom to continue with the survey.

God has the property of being the greatest conceivable being. He has infinite knowledge and unlimited power. He is present everywhere. He embodies perfect goodness, divine simplicity, and eternal existence. He is creator and sustainer of any universe there may be.

Source: *The Oxford Companion to Philosophy* (Honderich 2005)

According to the description, which attribute does God possess?
- He has infinite knowledge.
- He has perfect goodness.
- He has unlimited power.
- All of the above.

Outcome Questions

We would now like to ask for your opinion on some social issues. Please indicate the degree to which you agree or disagree with the following statements:

Wives should not have to do more housework than husbands do.
When jobs are scarce, men should have more right to a job than women.
Political parties should do more to encourage qualified women to run for political office.
On the whole, men make better political leaders than women do.
I do not want immigrants/foreign workers as neighbors.
Homosexual couples should have the right to marry one another.

(Answer options for each of the statements are: Strongly agree, Somewhat agree, Neither agree nor disagree, Somewhat disagree, Strongly disagree.)

3.2 Studies 2–4

Studies 2–4 were conducted in June 2019 on Lucid and are extensions of Study 1.[16] Lucid is a market research platform that provides access to survey respondents around the world. We used the nationally representative sample of US adults that Lucid provides through Fulcrum Academia, a platform for academic research. It is not a probability sample, but it achieves representativeness

---

[16] While Study 1 was exploratory, Studies 2–4 were pre-registered before data collection and the pre-analysis plan for these studies can be found at https://osf.io/s9npj/?view_on ly=ccc853b07f0b4f6b882febb9031793e1. These studies were approved by the Washington University Institutional Review Board, IRB ID # 201901194.

through quota sampling. For Studies 2–4, we have sample sizes of 1,197, 1,208, and 1,201, respectively, that is, about 600 respondents for each arm. Lucid provided sociodemographic data, including gender, age, education, ethnicity, household income, political ideology,[17] and region.

We designed these studies to accomplish three important extensions of Study 1: (1) to use counter-stereotypes in a political domain, (2) to examine the effect of men in counter-stereotypical roles, and (3) to perform a placebo test, that is, in the absence of gender stereotypes, we observe null effects on attitudes. Therefore, the manipulation in Study 2 examines a role in the political domain that has a strong masculine stereotype. In Study 3, we examine a role with a strong feminine stereotype, and in Study 4, a role that is gender-neutral.

Before carrying out the experiments, on July 9 and 15, 2018, we tested for gender associations of various roles on Amazon Mechanical Turk (MTurk). That is, we used MTurk to run tests that helped us design the experimental vignettes for Studies 2–4. Specifically, we were interested in finding (1) a role in the political domain that has a strong masculine stereotype, (2) a role with a strong feminine stereotype, and (3) a role that is gender-neutral. For the first, we thought of president, minister of defense, and lieutenant general as potential candidates. For the second, potential options were housekeeper, teacher, and parent. For the third, we thought of server, bartender, singer, and political party member. To choose from these options, we asked workers on MTurk to rate how strongly they associate each of the roles with males or females, with answer options ranging from "Strongly female" to "Strongly male" on a seven-point scale. Taking advantage of this opportunity, we also asked respondents to rate God, so that we can test whether our assumption for Study 1 that God is perceived as male is valid. Our data about God thus constitute a post-test rather than a pre-test.

We found that presidents have one of the strongest male associations, that housekeepers have one of the strongest female associations, and that singers are one of the most gender-neutral roles. Therefore, we used president in Study 2, housekeeper in Study 3, and singer in Study 4. In other words, based on these pre-tests, we picked president as the stereotypically male role, housekeeper as the stereotypically female role, and singer as a gender-neutral role. We also found that God is indeed considered more masculine than feminine, which confirms that God is indeed considered strongly male, as assumed in Study 1. Figure 1 shows distributions of responses for each of the four roles, with higher values on the horizontal axis meaning respondents rate the role as masculine.

---

[17] Our pre-registered covariate was *Party ID* with Republican, Democrat, Independent as response categories. Instead, Lucid provided a measure of political orientation that ranges from one to seven. We are thus forced to deviate slightly from the pre-registration by using a more granular measure of political leanings.

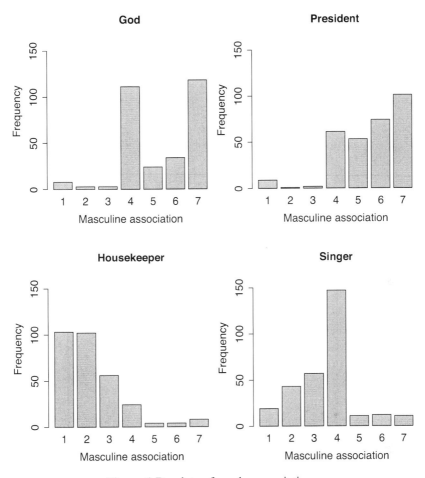

Figure 1 Barplots of gender associations.

Note: Barplots of MTurk respondents' ratings of the gender associations of God, president, housekeeper, and singer. The question asked "How strongly do you associate the following with males and females?" Responses range from one ("Strongly female") to seven ("Strongly male"). We asked each question to about 300 respondents.

To provide full information, Table 1 shows the distributions for all the other roles that we tested: masculine stereotypes (lieutenant general, president, minister of defense), feminine stereotypes (teacher, housekeeper, parent), and neutral roles (server, bartender, singer, political party member). The first section of the table illustrates that lieutenant general is considered slightly more male than president, but we chose to focus on presidents because the difference is minimal and because we preferred a more political (elected) position for Study 2. Defense minister had the lowest male-association, which is somewhat surprising given that defense is stereotypically a very masculine domain (Barnes and O'Brien 2018).

Table 1 Descriptive statistics for male-stereotype, female-stereotype,
and gender-neutral roles.

Variable	N	Min	q_1	Median	Mean	q_3	Max	SD
Lieutenant General	301	1	5	6	5.9	7	7	1.4
President	301	1	5	6	5.6	7	7	1.4
Defense minister	300	1	4	6	5.2	7	7	1.7
Teacher	301	1	1	2	2.2	3	7	1.3
Housekeeper	301	1	1	2	2.2	3	7	1.3
Parent	301	1	2	3	2.7	4	7	1.3
Server	300	1	2	4	3.4	4	7	1.4
Bartender	300	1	4	5	4.7	6	7	1.5
Singer	300	1	3	4	3.6	4	7	1.3
Party member	300	1	4	4	4.7	6	7	1.2

Note: q_1 indicates the first quartile; q_3 is the third quartile. SD stands for standard deviation.

The middle section of Table 1 shows the distributions for the a priori female-stereotype roles. Teacher and housekeeper had very similar distributions; we chose housekeeper by a coin toss. Parent, on the other hand, had the lowest female association. This, again, is interesting and indicates gender norms around parenting perhaps are not as rigid as gender stereotypes would presume (Tavits et al. 2024). It is also possible that since the word "parent" is often encouraged as an explicitly gender neutral term over mother/father, people have a slightly less female-biased view of the term compared to "teacher" and "housekeeper," which do not have alternative gender-specific options.

The last section of the table shows the distributions of gender-neutral roles. We can see that the distribution for singer is the most concentrated around the center. Servers are considered more female, while bartenders and party members tend to be more male. In short, our choice of the various roles that we used as part of our experimental treatments were not arbitrary but were guided by the results of these pre-tests.

A common feature of Studies 2–4 that further extends Study 1 is that the vignette includes visual in addition to textual treatment. Specifically, Study 2 randomizes vignettes that define presidents as either female (counter-stereotype) or male (stereotype) using a description of presidents around the world (rather than in reference to the US alone) with female/male pronouns and a picture of actual female/male presidents. We used pictures of the women presidents of the three Eastern European countries (Croatia, Estonia, Lithuania) from 2017 and the three male presidents of Bosnia and Herzegovina from 2014 to 2018. We use a definition of the role from an authoritative source, *Encyclopedia Britannica*. Study 3 defines housekeepers as male (counter-stereotype) or female (stereotype) using a description of housekeeper (from *U.S. News & World Report*) with male/female pronouns and a picture of a male/female housekeeper. Study 4 randomizes exposure to definitional information from CareersInMusic.com about singers (a gender-neutral role) in female or male terms, using text and a picture. We took great care to make sure that the visuals are equivalent across treatments. The two pictures used in each study are highly similar to each other except for gender. Appendix A1 presents the treatments we used and elaborates on our picture choices.

Again, consistent with Study 1, we reinforced the treatment in Studies 2–4 through a comprehension check question that followed the manipulation picture and text. A large share of respondents picked the correct answer: 67 percent, 74 percent, and 80 percent, for Studies 2–4, respectively. These passage rates are likely to be lower than in Study 1 because the content of Studies 2–4 is somewhat more technical than that of Study 1. Nonetheless, the main purpose of the comprehension question was to repeatedly expose respondents to the relevant gender pronouns used in the response options. Moreover, as with Study 1, the correct answer was "All of the above," meaning that other response options are technically correct as well.

Posttreatment, Studies 2–4 asked about respondents' views on gender and LGBTQ equality by including items *Housework*, *Parties*, *Leaders*, and *Gay* from Study 1. For LGBTQ equality, we included additional questions asking about agreement or disagreement with the following statements: "society has not gone far enough in accepting people who are transgender" (*Transgender*), and "someone can be a man or a woman even if that is different from the sex they were assigned at birth" (*Sex*). These question wordings are taken verbatim from the Pew Research Center Survey.[18] Answers to all questions are in a four-point scale. We chose these questions because we seek to understand the effects of counter-stereotypes about gender roles on gender- and LGBTQ-related attitudes generally.[19] In other words, we are testing whether female president treatment influences not only attitudes about women in the political domain, but also women in the nonpolitical domain and LGBTQ attitudes. Similarly, we explore whether the male housekeeper treatment affects gender

---

[18] https://www.pewresearch.org/social-trends/2022/06/28/americans-complex-views-on-gender-identity-and-transgender-issues/

[19] The *Gay* item measures attitudes about marriage between homosexuals, so it taps into attitudes about lesbian, gay, and bisexual people. The *Transgender* and *Sex* items measure attitudes about transgender people. None of our questions measure attitudes about queer people per se, but being queer means different things to different people, so we believe that our *Gay*, *Transgender*, and *Sex* items are good for measuring attitudes about the LGBTQ population broadly speaking.

attitudes in the home as well as gender attitudes in politics and attitudes about LGBTQ individuals.[20]

In terms of expected relationships, as was the case in Study 1, exposure to information about female presidents (Study 2) and a male housekeeper (Study 3) could weaken or suppress stereotypical associations, leading respondents to express more gender-equitable views at home, in workplace, and in politics. Such weaker binary views about gender roles could also lead respondents to view gender and sexuality in a less binary manner, resulting in more supportive views of marriage between two men or two women, and acceptance of transgender individuals.

3.3 Study 5

As discussed previously for Studies 1–4, we designed our treatments to be strong by reinforcing them in a number of ways (through texts, photos, and comprehension questions). However, one might argue that a single treatment still remains too weak. To address this, we fielded another separate study (N=1,199) that strengthens the treatments further by combining the (counter-)stereotypical depictions of God, presidents, and housekeepers and presenting them all to respondents in each condition.

The study was conducted from July 9 to July 10, 2021. The experiment has two treatment arms: stereotype and counter-stereotype. Stereotype treatment combines the stereotypical vignettes from Studies 1–3, that is, male depiction of God, male depiction of president, and female depiction of housekeeper. Counter-stereotype treatment combines the counter-stereotypical vignettes: female God, female president, and male housekeeper. Within experimental arm, the three vignettes were shown in random order. After treatment, respondents were asked about their views on gender and LGBTQ issues (*Housework*, *Parties*, *Leaders*, *Gay*, *Transgender*, and *Sex* variables) on a one to five scale. We have about 600 respondents per arm (total sample size: 1,199). We recruited US-based respondents on Prolific. Prolific is a research platform that was originally developed in the UK, but it has panelists from around the world, including the US. The study was preregistered before data collection, on June 13, 2021.[21]

---

[20] We did not include the *Neighbor* item in Studies 2–4 as well as Study 5, which will be described next. Since Study 1 yielded null effects of counter-stereotypical information on the main outcomes of interest, we did not see much value in including the placebo outcome question in subsequent studies.

[21] The pre-analysis plan can be found at https://osf.io/s9npj/?view_only=ccc853b07f0b4f6b882 febb9031793e1. The study was approved by the Washington University in St. Louis Institutional Review Board as a modification of the originally approved study, IRB ID # 201901194.

In conclusion, this section outlined the design principles of five experiments conducted to test the hypotheses regarding the effects of exposure to counter-stereotypes on attitudes about gender equality and LGBTQ rights. The experiments use a between-subjects design and are embedded in surveys, with both probability-based and non-probability-based samples of the US adult population. To achieve strong and realistic interventions, the treatments we use are of the sort encountered in the real world and easily implemented by policymakers. They use descriptions and visual stimuli, and signal acceptance and normality in the way that the descriptions are phrased and by citing those descriptions from authoritative sources. Additionally, the roles presented are perceived strongly counter-stereotypical and reinforced with comprehension questions. Table 2 summarizes the key features of our main five studies. Having provided an account of the design of each study and the rationale behind the choices made, we turn to analyzing the results in the next section.

4 Analyses and Results

This section presents the results of the five experiments. Before testing the effects of exposure to counter-stereotypes, we perform balance tests for each of our five studies to help ensure that randomization was successful and that the experimental groups are comparable on important characteristics. We then turn to presenting the results of the hypotheses tests, starting with Study 1 that uses counter-stereotypical versus stereotypical depictions of God. We then discuss the results of Studies 2 and 3, which use different counter-stereotypical exemplars, and Study 4, which serves as a placebo test. Finally, we present the results for Study 5, which uses the same vignettes about God, presidents, and housekeepers used in the first three experiments, but we strengthen treatment by presenting respondents with (counter-)stereotypical information on all of those roles, not just one of them.

4.1 Balance Tests

We begin by checking that there is balance between the experimental groups in each of our studies and that randomization was successful. First, we find that there are no systematic differences in the distributions of gender, age, household income, education level, race, political ideology, and region between the experimental arms. Using t-tests and chi-square tests, Appendix A2 shows that there is balance across Studies 1–5. The only case where there is significant difference is for the age variable in Study 3. Specifically, the average age of respondents is significantly higher in the female housekeeper condition than in the male housekeeper condition. Regarding randomization, for each study, we

Table 2 Summary of the five studies.

	Stereotype condition	Counter-stereotype condition	Sample	Sample size
Study 1	Male God	Female God	TAPS (probability)	2,111
Study 2	Male president	Female president	Lucid (non-probability)	1,197
Study 3	Female housekeeper	Male housekeeper	Lucid (non-probability)	1,208
Study 4	Placebo conditions using male and female singers (expectation: null effect)		Lucid (non-probability)	1,201
Study 5	Male God, male president, female housekeeper (all three presented in random order)	Female God, female president, male housekeeper (all three presented in random order)	Prolific (non-probability)	1,199

regress assignment into either experimental condition on the seven sociodemographic variables. As presented in Appendix A2, again the only predictor that has a statistically significant effect is the age variable in Study 3. We attribute this rare statistical significance to chance. Moreover, we do not see this as posing a problem for the results because if respondent age is higher in the female-housekeeper group and if that correlates with more gender-stereotypical views, we are more likely to observe more favorable attitudes toward gender equality and LGBTQ rights in the male-housekeeper (i.e., counter-stereotype) group. Yet we do not find statistically significant effects as will be discussed later. The appendix further shows that across studies, a likelihood ratio test indicates we cannot reject the null hypothesis that the coefficients are jointly zero.

4.2 Constructing the Variables

Next, we coded respondents' answers to each of the outcome questions so that higher values indicate more equitable attitudes. We will test treatment effects on each of the outcome questions separately. In addition, however, we created latent variables to measure broader attitudinal constructs. For Study 1, we averaged responses to (1) all questions about gender equality (variable name *Gender – all*), (2) questions about gender equality in politics (items *Parties* and *Leaders*; variable name *Gender – political*), and (3) questions about gender equality in the nonpolitical domain (items *Housework* and *Jobs*; variable name *Gender – social*). We created the first scale because it is useful to examine on-average attitudes about gender equality in all areas despite differences that can exist within. And since we have two questions on gender equality in politics, one question in the home, and one in the economy, we created the second scale for politics and the third scale to group the two nonpolitical questions together. For Studies 2–5, we averaged responses to (1) all questions about gender equality (*Gender – all*), (2) questions about gender equality in politics as defined above (*Gender – political*), and (3) all questions about LGBTQ equality (items *Gay, Transgender, Sex* ; variable name *LGBTQ*).[22] Again, we created the first scale because it is useful to examine on-average attitudes about gender equality in all areas. And since we left out the item *Job* that we had in Study 1, we have two politics-related gender items and only one non-politics-related gender item, which is why we created the second scale grouping the politics-related gender items. Lastly, Studies 2–5 have two more items in the LGBTQ

---

[22] Our pre-registration included slightly different variable names – the current versions are more concise. In addition, some of our latent variables differ from the pre-registered ones. Since we present the result for each item separately, this is inconsequential for drawing conclusions.

domain (i.e., *Transgender* and *Sex*), so it is useful to examine on-average attitudes about the LGBTQ by averaging those two items and the *Gay* variable.

The average Cronbach's alpha value of the *Gender – all* scale across the five studies is 0.59. For the *Gender – political* scale, the average alpha value is 0.54. The *Gender – social* scale, which is only relevant for Study 1, has an alpha value of 0.4. These are not high values, which indicate that people are aware of nuances in matters of gender equality, as one might expect. The average alpha value of the *LGBTQ* latent variables across Studies 2 to 5 is 0.79. The higher average for *LGBTQ* indicates that attitudes are indeed less nuanced in the newer domain of sexual and gender minorities. Similar patterns emerge using inter-item correlations. The average interitem correlation of all gender-related items across the five studies is 0.32. The average interitem correlation of all LGBTQ-related items across Studies 2–5 is 0.56. These figures justify our examination of treatment effects on both individual items and latent variables below.

As for the treatments, for Study 1 we code respondents who received the female-God treatment as "1" and those who received the male-God treatment as "0" (variable name: *Female God*). For Studies 2–4, we have binary variables named *Female president*, *Male housekeeper*, and *Female singer*. These variables take "1" if the respondent received the female-president, male-housekeeper, or female-singer treatment, respectively. For Study 5, we code respondents as "1" if they received vignette combining female-God, female-president, and male-housekeeper, and as "0" otherwise. For each study, we run t-tests with false discovery rate correction using the Benjamini–Hochberg procedure to account for multiple comparisons. This procedure controls for the false discovery rate and is a less stringent method of adjusting p-values compared to the Bonferroni correction. The latter assumes that all tests are independent from one another – something that is not the case for our studies.

4.3 Results for Study 1

The first panel of Figure 2 shows the difference in means and 95 percent confidence intervals for each single-item outcome variable (indicated on the horizontal axis) in Study 1. Difference in means is calculated by subtracting the mean of the outcome in the male-God group from that in the female-God group. Therefore, higher values indicate more equitable attitudes in the female-God group. Confidence intervals are calculated after correcting p-values for multiple comparisons.

The plot shows that the female-God treatment does not have a statistically significant effect on attitudes about gender or LGBTQ equality: the differences

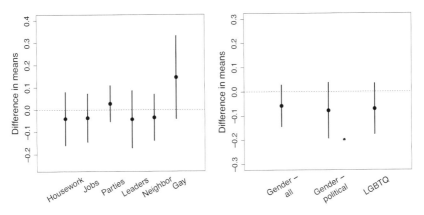

Figure 2 T-test results of study 1, with false discovery rate correction.

Note: Black circles show difference in means between the two treatment groups (female God – male God) for each outcome variable on the x-axis. Black lines show 95 percent confidence intervals. The confidence intervals have been adjusted for multiple comparison using the Benjamini–Hochberg procedure. The left-hand panel shows results for single-question outcome variables. The right-hand panel shows results for averaged outcome variables.

are indistinguishable from zero for all items. Although differences are in the anticipated direction for the gender item *Parties* and the LGBTQ item *Gay*, they are not statistically significant. Moreover, even if we were to test for meaningful effects rather than presence of effects (Rainey 2014), for *Parties*, the right end of the 90 percent confidence interval is 0.09, which is 10.02 percent of the standard deviation of the variable (0.95). For *Gay*, the right end of the confidence interval is 0.30, which is 20.82 percent of the standard deviation of the variable (1.44). Hence, the magnitude of any potential effects is small.

Overall, we do not have evidence that being exposed to counter-stereotypical information about gender roles moves gender and LGBTQ-related attitudes in a more equitable direction. The counter-stereotype treatment also does not have an effect on attitudes about immigrants (*Neighbor*). This is a placebo outcome, where we expected null effects.

These null results across outcomes continue to hold for analyses using latent variables, as shown in the second panel of Figure 2. The directions of the coefficients are, in fact, negative. This is interesting and in line with the possibility that counter-stereotypical treatments, instead of encouraging equitable attitudes, could actually backfire. The more mixed results from the left-hand panel of Figure 2, and the fact that all the coefficients on the latent variable are not significant, make difficult to read too much into the negative coefficients. However, it is an interesting observation to note.

4.4 Results for Studies 2–4

Recall that for Studies 2–4, the counter-stereotypical treatment focuses on female presidents, a male housekeeper, and a female singer, respectively, with the last study (Study 4) serving as a placebo. As we explain later, even with all of these different treatments, we continue to find similar null results as with the female God treatment in Study 1.

First, Figure 3 shows the results for Study 2. As with Figure 2, the plots show results for single-item (left) and latent (right) outcomes. Difference in means is calculated by subtracting the mean of the outcome in the male-president group from that in the female-president group, so that higher values indicate more equitable attitudes in the female-president group. The first panel of Figure 3 shows that the female-president treatment does not have a statistically significant effect on attitudes about gender equality, and about sexual and gender minorities. The results are null regardless of whether the outcome is more proximal to the political treatment (e.g., *Parties*, *Leaders*) or not (e.g., *Housework*). The difference is in the anticipated direction for *Gay*, but it is very small and not statistically significant. Even if we think in terms of testing for meaningful effects (Rainey 2014), the positive end of the 90 percent confidence interval is 0.11, which is 9.73 percent of the standard deviation of the variable (1.08).

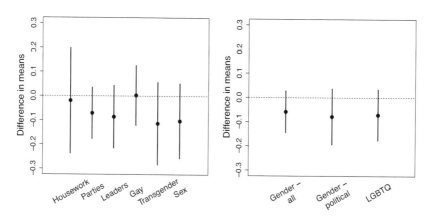

Figure 3 T-test results of study 2, with false discovery rate correction.

Note: Black circles show difference in means between the two treatment groups (female president – male president) for each outcome variable on the x-axis. Black lines show 95 percent confidence intervals. The confidence intervals have been adjusted for multiple comparison using the Benjamini–Hochberg procedure. The left-hand panel shows results for single-question outcome variables. The right-hand panel shows results for averaged outcome variables.

And again, averaging across multiple items does not change the results as shown in the second panel of Figure 3. Note again, however, that the directions of the coefficients are negative, as was the case with Study 1. Here, the negative coefficients are more consistently present across both panels of Figure 3, suggesting again a possible backfire effect. Still, the effects never reach the level of statistical significance, making it hard to draw firm conclusions about the direction of the effect. All in all, we conclude that the null result in Study 1 is not an artifact of a nonpolitical domain covered in that study but extends to the political realm of Study 2.

Figure 4 shows the results for Study 3. Difference in means is calculated by subtracting the mean of the outcome in the female-housekeeper group from that in the male-housekeeper group. That is, higher values indicate more equitable attitudes in the male-housekeeper group. Again, all individual outcomes in the left panel show null results. The differences for the gender item *Housework* and all the LGBTQ items (*Gay*, *Transgender*, and *Sex*) are positive – the anticipated direction – but not reliable.

The right panel reveals the same patterns. Even when all gender or political gender outcomes are averaged, there is no reliable difference between the female- and male- housekeeper groups. When the LGBTQ outcomes are averaged, although the difference is positive with a value of 0.07, it is not statistically significant. In terms of meaningful effects (Rainey 2014), the positive end

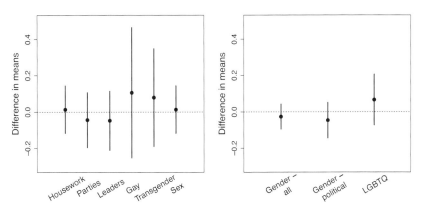

Figure 4 T-test results of study 3, with false discovery rate correction.

Note: Black circles show difference in means between the two treatment groups (male housekeeper – female housekeeper) for each outcome variable on the x-axis. Black lines show 95 percent confidence intervals. The confidence intervals have been adjusted for multiple comparison using the Benjamini–Hochberg procedure. The left-hand panel shows results for single-question outcome variables. The right-hand panel shows results for averaged outcome variables.

of the 90 percent confidence interval is 0.18, which is just 19.32 percent of the standard deviation of LGBTQ (0.95).

In sum, the results for Study 3 suggest that the null results from Studies 1 and 2 are not because those studies portray women in counter-stereotypical roles. Null results extend to examples of men in counter-stereotypical roles. Note however, that unlike Studies 1 and 2, the coefficients here are scattered more firmly around zero and do not leave an impression of a backfire effect. In fact, several coefficients are actually positive, that is, in the hypothesized direction. Again, since none of them reach the level of statistical significance, we cannot draw firm conclusions. But digging further into the possibility that seeing women in counter-stereotypical roles potentially backfire (Studies 1 and 2) when seeing men in such roles does not is an interesting task for future studies.

Lastly, Figure 5 shows the results for Study 4, the placebo test. Difference in means subtracts the mean of the outcome in the male-singer group from that in the female-singer group so that higher values indicate more equitable attitudes in the female-singer group. The left panel shows that there is no difference in the single-item outcomes across the two groups. Although attitudes tend to be more equitable in the female-singer group, as seen by the positive differences, they are not statistically significant. Moreover, the right-hand panel shows that the null results hold for all averaged variables. These null results are expected, given the absence of gender stereotypes in the design of Study 4.

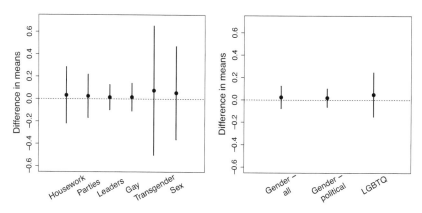

Figure 5 T-test results of study 4, with false discovery rate correction.

Note: Black circles show difference in means between the two treatment groups (female singer treatment – male singer treatment) for each outcome variable. Black lines show 95 percent confidence intervals. The confidence intervals have been adjusted for multiple comparison using the Benjamini–Hochberg procedure. The left-hand panel shows results for single-question outcome variables. The right-hand panel shows results for averaged outcome variables.

All in all, the results of Studies 2–4 are consistent with the result of Study 1. While there is much theoretical and practical reason to anticipate that exposure to counter-stereotypical gender roles will increase more equitable attitudes about women and sexual and gender minorities, we do not have evidence of such effects.

Moreover, the results from Studies 1 and 2 suggest that, if anything, counter-stereotypical treatments could have a tendency to backfire. As we can see in the right-hand side plots in Figures 2 and 3, the difference in means is negative (although not statistically significant) in most cases, i.e., average attitudes are usually more inequitable among respondents who received the counter-stereotypical vignette. One possible explanation is that counter-stereotypical information sits uncomfortably for some respondents and thus has tendencies to worsen the equitability of attitudes. As we will show in the next section, there is slight evidence among some subsets of respondents that counter-stereotypical treatments can actually reduce support for gender equality and LGBTQ rights. Such findings are not consistent and are rarely statistically significant so we cannot read much into them, but they add to the overall result that there is no evidence of counter-stereotypical gender roles *increasing* tolerable attitudes about gender and LGBTQ issues.

4.5 Results for Study 5

The treatment for Study 5 combines female-God, female-president, and male-housekeeper treatments, thereby presumably delivering a "higher dose" of counter-stereotypical information about gender roles. This study addresses the potential concern that the treatments in Studies 1, 2, and 3 are not strong enough. Figure 6 presents the results of Study 5. It shows t-test results with p-values adjusted for multiple comparisons. All the outcome variables shown on the x-axis are constructed the same way as in the previous studies: individual items on the left panel and averaged variables on the right panel. Difference in means subtracts the mean of the outcome in the stereotype group from that in the counter-stereotype group so that higher values indicate more equitable attitudes in the counter-stereotype group.

Despite the possibility that the high-dose treatment would have a stronger effect on gender and LGBTQ attitudes, the results do not show any significant differences between the treatment group and the control group. Not only are these differences not statistically significant, but they are also generally minimal in size. This is especially the case for outcomes related to the LGBTQ population. The mean is higher in the counter-stereotypical group for both *Transgender* and *Sex* variables, but the difference in the *Transgender* variables

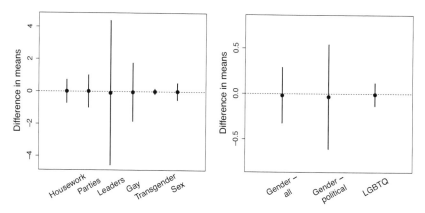

Figure 6 T-test results of study 5, with false discovery rate correction.

Note: Black circles show difference in means between the two treatment groups (counterstereotype – stereotype) for each outcome variable on the x-axis. Black lines show 95 percent confidence intervals. The confidence intervals have been adjusted for multiple comparison using the Benjamini–Hochberg procedure. The left-hand panel shows results for single-question outcome variables. The right-hand panel shows results for averaged outcome variables.

is 0.003 and the difference in the *Sex* variables is 0.01. When it comes to the *Gay* variable, the mean for the stereotypical group is higher and the difference is −0.03. Among the outcomes related to gender equality, the largest difference is observed for the *Leader* variable, with the mean being lower by 0.085 in the counter-stereotype group.

With respect to the averaged outcome variables shown on the right panel of Figure 6, again the differences are not statistically significant. The means are all higher for the stereotype experimental group. The difference in means for the overall gender variable is −0.017, the political gender variable is −0.03, and the LGBTQ variable is −0.007.

These results suggest that even when presented with an intensified treatment of counter-stereotypical information, attitudes about gender and LGBTQ rights may be difficult to change. It suggests that the null findings in Studies 1–3 are not likely because the treatment was weak. Study 5 further highlights that the role of counter-stereotypes in undermining prejudice might be more complex than we originally anticipated.

4.6 Robustness and Conclusions

We checked that all these results across Studies 1–5 are robust to alternative modeling strategies, including ordinary least squares (OLS) with sociodemographic controls and imbalanced pre-treatment covariates, and ordinal logit with and without sociodemographic controls. We also conducted t-tests without adjusting for multiple comparisons, as they are conservative tests of null findings.

In Appendix A3, we present these results, specifically using single-question outcome variables in Studies 1–3 and 5. Figures A1–A4 show the results for Studies 1–3 and 5, respectively. To clarify, for each study, we ran (1) linear regressions, controlling for sociodemographic covariates, (2) linear regressions, controlling for imbalanced covariates where they exist, (3) ordinal logit models without any controls, and (4) ordinal logit models with sociodemographic covariates. All models are adjusted for multiple comparisons using false discovery rate correction. In addition, we ran our main t-tests without false discovery rate correction. Results are consistently null except when we do the t-test without adjusting p-values for the gay marriage outcome (*Gay*) in Study 1 (see the last panel of Figure A1). Considering that this is the only case where we find a significant effect and it is suboptimal to not adjust p-values for multiple comparisons, the overall results demonstrate the robustness of our main null findings.

Furthermore, we conducted mini meta-analyses to check whether the null results hold when we aggregate the data across studies to increase statistical power (Goh et al. 2016). Mini meta-analysis allows us to check whether our null results are because of imprecision or not. It calculates Cohen's *d* values and their 95 percent confidence intervals. We did mini meta-analysis for three outcome variables that are common across Studies 1, 2, 3, and 5: *Gender – all, Gender – political*, and *Gay*. They measure averaged responses to all gender questions, averaged responses to political gender questions only, and responses to the question of gay marriage. We also did mini meta-analysis for *LGBTQ*, which measures averaged responses to the LGBTQ items, using Studies 2, 3, and 5 where we measured that variable. Because the scales of the variables vary across studies, meta-analyses were conducted using results obtained after rescaling each variable for each study to range from zero to one.

As shown in Figure 7, we find that the difference between treatment groups is not statistically significant across all outcomes: *Gender – all* ($d = -0.05$, 95% CI: [−0.10, 0.01]), *Gender – political* ($d = -0.05$, 95% CI: [−0.10, 0.00]), *Gay* ($d = 0.048$, 95% CI: [−0.00, 0.10]), and *LGBTQ* ($d = -0.00$, 95% CI: [−0.07, 0.06]). Therefore, we conclude that our main findings are robust – there is no evidence of difference between the responses of the stereotype group and the counter-stereotype group. Our results are not an artifact of lack of power.

In conclusion, we examined the effect of counter-stereotypical information on gender and LGBTQ attitudes using five sets of treatments in Studies 1–5. The results show that, despite the various treatments, the counter-stereotypical

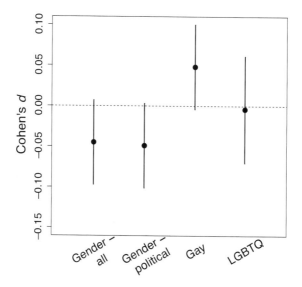

Figure 7 Mini meta-analysis results.

Note: The results for *Gender – all*, *Gender – political*, and *Gay* outcomes use the results of Studies 1, 2, 3, and 5. The result for *LGBTQ* uses findings from Studies 2, 3, and 5. Black circles show Cohen's *d* values. Black lines show their 95 percent confidence intervals. We present the results of fixed effects analysis, which is more appropriate when the composite studies are similar to each other methodologically and the focus is on analyzing those studies rather than generalizing beyond (Goh et al. 2016).

information did not have a statistically significant effect on attitudes toward gender or LGBTQ equality. The null results are consistent across all studies and are not an artifact of political or nonpolitical domains. Additionally, combining the treatments in Study 5 to deliver a higher dose of counter-stereotypical information did not yield any significant results. These findings are puzzling in light of our theory that draws on well-established arguments across literatures in a number of fields as well as the real-life relevance of the kinds of normalized counter-stereotypes we used. In the next section, we explore some of the potential reasons behind the null findings in order to shed more light on why counter-stereotypical information night have not been effective in changing attitudes about gender equality and attitudes about sexual and gender minorities.

5 Why the Null Results?

Given the theoretical and practical backing of our expectations and the strong experimental treatments that simulate counter-stereotypical information that people encounter in everyday contexts, it is important to understand why we have null results. Therefore, we explored several possibilities to try to understand the reasons behind these results. We discuss first the explanations that do not seem to hold for our research and then turn to the explanation that seems to explain our findings.

5.1 Are the Results Masking Subgroup Effects?

First, one might ask whether the counter-stereotype treatments in Studies 1–3 and 5 have effects on subgroups of respondents in our data. The counter-stereotype treatments could have positive effects on the equitability of attitudes among some subgroups of respondents while having null or negative effects on equitable attitudes among other groups. In particular, there may be variation in results by gender, education level, and ideology. Starting with gender, it might be the case that counter-stereotypes are effective for women as opposed to men. Women, as the subjects of marginalization and inequality, might be more alert and responsive to cues about counter-stereotypes than men. Second, it might be that the less educated are more likely to be affected. If it is the case that the less educated are more susceptible to new information and manipulable, then they might be more likely to express equitable and tolerant attitudes after being primed to think counter-stereotypically about gender roles. Highly educated respondents, on the other hand, might be more resistant to updating their previous attitudes. However, expectations about education can go in the other direction as well. Highly educated respondents might in fact be able to learn better in that they are better able to connect counter-stereotypical information with their existing attitudes. According to this logic, higher level of education means more likelihood of expressing equitable attitudes after counter-stereotype treatment. Lastly, it might be that there are differences for people of different ideologies. Left-wing voters, who in general tend to be socially and cognitively open and flexible (e.g., Bakker et al. 2015; Jung and Tavits 2021b), might be more open to counter-stereotypical information compared to right-wing voters.[23]

To test for these possibilities with Studies 1–3 and 5, we first performed a series of interaction analyses by gender. For each of the single-item outcome variables, we ran a linear regression model with an interaction between an

---

[23] One might ask whether respondents reacted differently to treatment depending on their prior attitudes (see Boysen and Vogel 2007). For example, did respondents with prior inequitable attitudes express even more negative attitudes after being exposed to counter-stereotypical information? We do not have pre-treatment measures of outcome variables and cannot address the question directly. But if we assume that there are strong correlations between respondents' gender and attitudes about gender equality and between respondents' ideology and attitudes about LGBTQ rights, our analyses by gender and ideology help answer the question. As will be explained in later paragraphs, the results indicate that backfiring effects are possible but certainly not prevalent.

indicator for the counter-stereotype treatment and an indicator for the gender of the respondent, as well as their constituent terms. Second, we performed our analyses with interactions using education level. For each outcome variable, we ran a linear regression model with an interaction between an indicator for the counter-stereotype treatment and a continuous education variable, as well as and their constituent terms. Third, we ran similar models including interactions with respondents' left-right self-placement.

Figures A5–A8 in Appendix A4 show the gender interaction analyses for Studies 1–3 and 5, respectively. In each analysis, we use the single-item outcome variables. All in all, we do not find evidence of positive subgroup effects. In none of the analyses is the effect positive and statistically significant for male or female respondents. If anything, we find some significant negative effects among sub-groups. In particular, the counter-stereotypical president treatment in Study 2 has a negative effect on *Leaders* and *Sex* among female respondents, and the combined counter-stereotypical treatment in Study 5 has negative effects on *Leaders* and *Transgender* for male respondents. Yet, among these cases, the negative effect is significantly different from the null effect for the other subgroup only in the analysis where we examine the effect of the counter-stereotype treatment on the *Transgender* outcome variable in Study 5. There, we find a negative effect of counter-stereotype treatment on *Transgender* among male respondents, and it is significantly different from the null effect of treatment on the outcome among female respondents. In all other cases, the "backfiring" effects are not statistically distinguishable from the comparable null effect.[24] In short, there is no case of subgroup positive effects. While we do not report them in this Element, we also ran the same interaction models for the averaged outcome variables, and we continue to find substantively the same results. We also ran Kolmogorov–Smirnov tests to see if there are any differences in distributions of the averaged scales for female and male respondents separately. We do not find any significant differences between the stereotype and counter-stereotype groups.

Similar findings hold for interaction models using education. Figures A9–A12 in Appendix A5 show the results for Studies 1–3 and 5, respectively. We focus on single-item outcome variables. In none of the analyses is the marginal

---

[24] Future research could explore properly the potential for backfiring effects. Considering the finding that counter-stereotypical information presented in Study 5 reduces the attitude that "society has not gone far enough" on transgender issues (*Transgender*) among male respondents, one could conduct a study to see if the provision of normalized, matter-of-fact counter-stereotypical information reduces the attitude that *society* should do more for equality in a given domain. Perhaps this kind of treatment conveys the idea that sufficient efforts and progresses are being made in society. To test this, the outcome questions should be fixed in terms of issue area (e.g., transgender rights) and varied in terms of whether they measure perceptions of societal progress on the issue or respondents' personal views of it.

effect of counter-stereotype treatment positive and statistically significant across education levels. Again, we find some negative marginal effects instead. Specifically, the female-president treatment in Study 2 has negative effects on *Parties* among respondents with higher education levels. In this and only in this analysis, the interaction term between education and counter-stereotype treatment is negative and statistically significant.[25] This indicates that a backfiring effect is possible, similar to what we found in some of the analyses by gender discussed previously. But importantly, we do not observe counter-stereotypical treatment ever increasing equitable attitudes. When we run the same interaction models for averaged outcome variables in Studies 1–3 and 5, we again find similar results overall. We also ran Kolmogorov–Smirnov tests to see if there are any differences in distributions of the averaged scales for low- and high-education groups separately. We do not find any differences, other than less skewed (i.e., *less* equitable) distributions of *Gender – political* and *LGBTQ* for the counter-stereotype treatment group in Study 2 among the highly educated, which are respondents with median level of education or above.

Finally, Figures A13–A15 in Appendix A6 show the ideology interaction analyses for Studies 1–3, using the single-item outcome questions. Study 5 did not include a variable for political ideology, which is why we only focus on the first three studies in that section. The variable *Ideology* takes higher values for right-wing voters, ranging from one to seven. Again, in none of the analyses do we find a significant positive effect of counter-stereotype treatment. We do find some conditional negative effects, i.e., backfiring effects. Specifically, the female-God treatment in Study 1 has negative effects on *Job* and *Neighbor* outcome variables for conservative respondents; the female-president treatment in Study 2 has negative effects on *Transgender* among liberal respondents. Yet none of the interaction terms between counter-stereotype treatment and left-right attitudes is statistically significant. Therefore, the important takeaway from these analyses is that we do not find counter-stereotype treatments increasing equitable attitudes. Substantively similar results hold when we run the ideology interaction models for latent, averaged outcome variables in Studies 1–3. We also ran Kolmogorov–Smirnov tests to see if there are any differences in distributions of the averaged scales for liberal and conservative respondents separately, excluding respondents with the middle value in the *Ideology* variable. We do not find any differences between treatment groups.

Overall, we do not find any evidence of counter-stereotype treatment increasing equitable attitudes among subgroups of respondents. If anything, there is at

---

[25] This result also alleviates the potential concern that the overall null results presented in the last section are driven by the highly educated providing socially desirable responses (Clifford and Jerit 2015).

times a tendency for counter-stereotypical treatments to backfire and decrease equitable attitudes for some respondents. In short, these analyses alleviate the concern that our overall null results presented in Section 4 are masking subgroup effects.

5.2 Are the Null Results Due to Ceiling Effects?

One might ask whether the null results in Studies 1–3 and 5 are because of ceiling effects, i.e., because most respondents hold very equitable views about gender and the LGBTQ population to begin with or are willing to express very equitable attitudes due to social desirability concerns. To check this, we examined the distributions of our single-item outcome variables across all five experimental studies.

Figure A16 in Appendix A7 shows the distributions for the six outcome questions in Study 1. We see that, overall, the distributions are often skewed toward the left, as one would expect, but that there is not an over-concentration of responses in the higher end of the scale. This is especially the case for *Gay*, which makes sense since attitudes about sexual minorities are arguably more controversial and therefore more varied. The same holds for Figures A17–A19, which show the distributions of outcome questions in Studies 2, 3, and 5, respectively. Distributions are skewed toward the left. But what is different from Study 1 is that the *Gay* variable is skewed at similar levels to the gender-related outcomes, while *Transgender* and *Sex* are relatively less skewed than the gender-related outcomes. These patterns indicate that, as one would expect, attitudes about the transgender community and gender minorities are newer and more varied than attitudes about sexual minorities. The average standard deviation of outcomes in each study is around one. In short, it seems that ceiling effects are unlikely to be the cause of the overall null effects of counter-stereotypical treatments, considering there is reasonable variation in all outcome variables.[26]

5.3 Were the Treatments Too Strong and Thus Dismissed?

Some prior work suggests that when seeing strongly counter-stereotypical examples, individuals may conclude that they are exceptions. Rather than updating or weakening stereotypes as we argued in the theory section, such strong counter-stereotypes may lead to new cognitive categories, or subtypes, without changing the original stereotype (e.g., Allport 1954; Kunda and Oleson 1995, 1997; Weber and Crocker 1983). The concept of subtyping, however, is

---

[26] Note that the concern about demand effects (or spuriousness) does not apply in our case because we have null findings and not positive effects, that need to be explained.

not *directly* relevant to our studies. Our experiments here are different from the kinds of experiments used in previous work in social psychology because we are changing the stereotype of a role, not a particular figure. Unlike, for example, psychological research that uses atypical depictions of a particular lawyer named Steve to change stereotypes about lawyers in general (Kunda and Oleson 1995), we are presenting normalized counter-stereotypical information about presidents in general, housekeepers in general, and God. In other words, our counter-stereotypical treatments are matter-of-fact and normalized presentations rather than exemplars that focus on one specific individual in society. Our treatments do not present counter-stereotypical information in an "exceptional" way. That said, the general idea behind subtyping is still relevant to our studies because our overall null results might be due to the fact that the counter-stereotypical exemplars we used did not change respondents' *generalized* stereotypes about gender roles. As will be explained later, we did a follow-up study that gets at this question.

Alternatively, one might ask whether our respondents simply dismissed and rejected the counter-stereotypical treatments for being unrealistic and unusual. We do not think this is likely since female descriptions of God and presidents and male descriptions of housekeepers are rare but not impossible. Furthermore, the partial evidence of backfiring effects that we found and discussed in the earlier part of this section suggests that respondents did not necessarily abandon the counter-stereotypical information they saw. Counter-stereotypical information was impactful enough for some respondents such that they express less equitable/tolerant attitudes. The follow-up study we present later will also show that people do not simply dismiss and reject counter-stereotypical information.

An alternative perspective suggests that a striking (socially accepted) counter-stereotype, like the ones we use, may signal to the respondent that gender equality has been achieved and there is no need for further progress. In line with this, Georgeac and Rattan (2019) show that progress in the representation of women in leadership positions undermines support for further gender equality. Similar results have been reported on racial prejudice (Valentino and Brader 2011). Furthermore, strong counter-stereotypes that get interpreted as sign of progress could serve as a "moral license" for people to express opposition for further progress (Effron et al. 2009). These are plausible arguments. However, they are not helpful for explaining our overall null findings. First, empirically, they predict a clear negative treatment effect. When analyzing all respondents, some of the differences in means that we report in the previous section are negative in direction, but none are meaningfully and reliably so. When analyzing subgroups of respondents, we did find a couple of instances of negative effects, but they were neither consistent nor prevalent. Second, theoretically, such arguments about resistance to more equitability upon observance of equitability are not as relevant for attitudes about the LGBTQ. While learning, say, about female presidents may be interpreted as a sign of progress in gender equality, it does not necessarily communicate the same about progress in LGBTQ equality.

5.4 Did the Treatments Alter Stereotypes about Gender Roles?

The strength of the treatment aside, perhaps the type or nature of the treatments that we used failed to have the desired effect of diluting stereotypes about gender roles, i.e., the manipulation did not work. Alternatively, even if the manipulation worked in that it loosened the gender associations of the specific roles depicted in the counter-stereotypical examples, it is possible that this effect did not generalize outside of these specific examples. Using the role of the president as an example, while respondents may no longer as strongly associate presidency with males after seeing the female president treatment, their generic core beliefs about men and women may have remained unaltered. This may be why we do not see any significant effects on attitudes, which are likely reflecting generic beliefs rather than role-specific stereotypes.

To test this, we ran a follow-up experiment (N=3,600) where respondents were randomly assigned to one of the six experimental arms from Studies 1–3. This was followed by two sets of items: (1) questions probing respondents' gender association of the role presented in the treatment (i.e., questions that serve as a manipulation check), and (2) items measuring generic beliefs about men and women, which are reflected in the extent to which respondents think a set of particular adjectives describe men and women (Huddy and Terkildsen 1993).

In other words, our follow-up study explores the reasons for the null results in the main analyses by testing (a) whether the counter-stereotypical treatments from Studies 1–3 reduced stereotypical gender associations of the role depicted in the treatment and (b) whether those treatments alter respondents' generic core beliefs about women and men, i.e., whether they reduce more fundamental, generalizable gender trait stereotypes (Huddy and Terkildsen 1993) that extend beyond the specific roles presented in the treatments.

The follow-up experiment has six treatment arms: male God, female God, male president, female president, female housekeeper, and male housekeeper. These are exactly the same as in Studies 1–3. After respondents read one of the randomly assigned vignettes, they answer the following question: "How strongly do you associate the following with male or female?" Below the question, they saw *God*, *president*, or *housekeeper*, depending on the vignette that they received. Answer options ranged from "Strongly male" to "Strongly female" on a seven-point scale. After that question, we asked respondents two matrix-format questions that measure generic core beliefs (or gender trait stereotypes) about women and men separately. Specifically, we ask "How well do each of the following adjectives describe [*women/men*]?" The part in brackets was assigned in random order. The adjectives were also presented in random order and included "assertive," "tough," "rational," "self-confident," "warm," "gentle," "emotional," and "cautious." Four of these are stereotypically masculine (assertive, tough, rational, self-confident) and the remaining four are stereotypically feminine traits (warm, gentle, emotional, cautious). Answer options range from "Extremely well" to "Not well at all" on a five-point scale. This between-subjects experiment was conducted on 3,600 US-based respondents on Prolific from July 22 to July 23, 2021. There were about 600 respondents per treatment arm. Participant in this study do not overlap with participants from our other studies. This follow-up study was pre-registered as well.[27]

Figure 8 shows the results of t-tests for the first set of outcome questions, separately for the God, president, and housekeeper vignettes. Outcome variables range from one to seven, such that higher values indicate more stereotypical gender associations (i.e., associating God more with male than female, associating president more with male than female, associating housekeeper more with female than male). We find statistically significant negative effects. This means that respondents who received counter-stereotypical information are less likely to express stereotypical gender associations about that specific role. We conclude that the manipulation worked as expected: the treatments diluted stereotypes about gender roles.[28]

Figures 9–11 show t-test results for the second set of outcome questions on respondents' generic beliefs about women and men. We create outcome variables

---

[27] See https://osf.io/s9npj/?view_only=ccc853b07f0b4f6b882febb9031793e1. The study was approved by the Washington University in St. Louis Institutional Review Board as a modification of the originally approved study, IRB ID # 201901194.

[28] It is certainly possible that at least some respondents who received counter-stereotypical information responded in a counter-stereotypical way because of social desirability or a Hawthorne effect, i.e., because they saw information that is counter-stereotypical and believed they are expected to conform. However, we are not very worried about such insincere responses for two reasons. First, while stereotypical role assessments are significantly lower in the counter-stereotype groups compared to the stereotype groups as shown in Figure 8, the mean ratings in the counter-stereotype groups are still rather stereotypical. The mean is 4.93 in the female-God group, which is above the middle value of four ("Neither male nor female") and slightly less than five ("Slightly male"). The mean in the female-president group is 5.09, which is in between "Slightly male" (5) and "Moderately male" (6). The mean in the male-housekeeper group is 5.42, which is in between "Slightly female" (5) and "Moderately female" (6). Second, prior research shows that demand effects in survey experiments are rare (Mummolo and Peterson 2018).

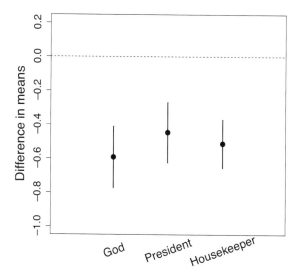

Figure 8 T-test results of follow-up experiment, gender associations.

Note: Black circles show difference in means between the two treatment groups (counterstereotype – stereotype) for each set of experimental arms (i.e., God experiment, president experiment, housekeeper experiment). Black lines show 95 percent confidence intervals. Outcome variables have been coded such that higher values indicate more stereotypical gender associations. The negative differences shown in the figure indicate that respondents who received the counter-stereotypical treatment express lower levels of stereotypical gender associations for God, president, and housekeeper, respectively.

that indicate more stereotypical beliefs for higher values. For example, higher values on *Assertive* for women mean that respondents are more likely to say that the word "assertive" does not describe women well. Another example is *Confident* for men, which takes higher values when respondents say that the word "confident" describes men well. The same logic goes for stereotypically feminine adjectives, such as "emotional": higher values of *Emotional* for women mean that respondents think the word describes women well, while higher values of *Emotional* for men mean that respondents think the word does not describe men well. All t-test results adjust p-values for multiple comparison.

Left panel of Figure 9 shows the effect of the female-God treatment (over the male-God treatment) on generic beliefs about women. Right panel of Figure 9 shows the effect of the female-God treatment (over the male-God treatment) on generic beliefs about men. Higher values on the outcome variable indicate more stereotypical beliefs about the sex in question. So negative (positive) differences indicate less (more) stereotypical beliefs among respondents in the female-God treatment group. While most of the differences are negative in direction, the effect sizes are small and not statistically significant.

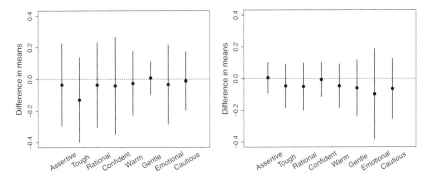

Figure 9 T-test results of follow-up, trait stereotypes about women and men (god treatments).

Note: Black circles show difference in means between the two treatment groups (female God – male God) for each outcome variable on the x-axis. Black lines show 95 percent confidence intervals. The confidence intervals have been adjusted for multiple comparison using the Benjamini–Hochberg procedure. Higher values on the outcome variable indicate more stereotypical gender trait associations for women (left) and men (right). In the left panel, negative (positive) differences indicate less (more) stereotypical trait associations among respondents in the female-God treatment group. In the right panel, negative (positive) differences indicate less (more) stereotypical trait associations among respondents in the female-God treatment group.

Figure 10 shows results for the effect of the female-president treatment (over the male-president treatment) on beliefs about women and men, respectively. Figure 11 shows results for the effect of the male-housekeeper treatment (over the female-housekeeper treatment) on beliefs about women and men, respectively. Outcome variables are similarly constructed such that higher values indicate more gender stereotypical beliefs, regardless of whether the question is about men or women. Negative (positive) differences in means indicate that respondents in the counter-stereotypical treatment group express lower (higher) levels of stereotypical generic beliefs than those in the stereotypical treatment group. For all these analyses, we consistently find null results with variation in the direction of the differences. That is, respondents' generic core beliefs associated with women and men do not change in response to seeing women and men in counter-stereotypical roles.

Put together, in the follow-up study, we find evidence that our counter-stereotype treatments reduce gender associations for the role depicted in the treatment, but no evidence that they reduce the generic core beliefs associated with women and men. We believe this is most likely why our counter-stereotype treatments have null effects on attitudes about gender equality and LGBTQ rights.

In other words, we find that the counter-stereotype treatments indeed increase counter-stereotypical gender associations of the role of interest, suggesting that

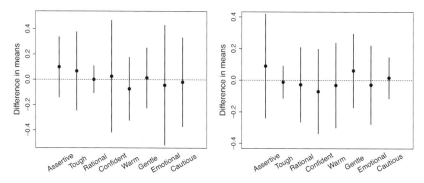

Figure 10 T-test results of follow-up, trait stereotypes about women and men
(president treatments).

Note: Black circles show difference in means between the two treatment groups (female
president – male president) for each outcome variable on the x-axis. Black lines show
95 percent confidence intervals. The confidence intervals have been adjusted for multiple
comparison using the Benjamini–Hochberg procedure. Higher values on the outcome
variable indicate more stereotypical gender trait associations about women (left) and men
(right). On the left panel, negative (positive) differences indicate less (more) stereotypical
trait associations among respondents in the female-president treatment group. On the right
panel, negative (positive) differences indicate less (more) stereotypical trait associations
among respondents in the female-president treatment group.

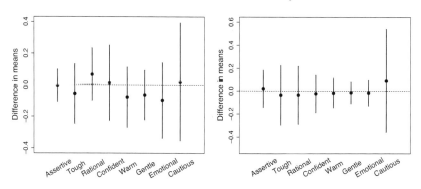

Figure 11 T-test results of follow-up, trait stereotypes about women and men
(housekeeper treatments).

Note: Black circles show difference in means between the two treatment groups (male
housekeeper – female house keeper) for each outcome variable on the x-axis. Black lines
show 95 percent confidence intervals. The confidence intervals have been adjusted for
multiple comparison using the Benjamini–Hochberg procedure. Higher values on the
outcome variable indicate more stereotypical gender trait associations about women (left)
and men (right). On the left panel, negative (positive) differences indicate less (more)
stereotypical trait associations among respondents in the male-housekeeper treatment
group. On the right panel, negative (positive) differences indicate less (more) stereotypical
trait associations among respondents in the male-housekeeper treatment group.

the manipulation worked as intended. This is important because it further undermines the potential concern that respondents dismissed the counter-stereotypical treatments for being unrealistic or that the counter-stereotypes that we use are meaningless for prejudice reduction.

However, respondents' generic beliefs about women and men remained unaffected, which most likely explains the null effects on gender-related attitudes in Studies 1–3 and 5. We interpret the broader implications of these findings as follows. First, they confirm that stereotypes are hard to change – psychological processes, from self-views to social acceptance, make any correctional efforts cognitively demanding (Ellemers 2018; Finnegan et al. 2015; see also Jung and Tavits 2021a; Tankard and Paluck 2017). In fact, a recent study shows that gender attitudes can persist throughout centuries (Damann et al. 2023). Second, they suggest that the kind of brief and passive exposure to counter-stereotypes that people experience in everyday life, which is the context our survey experiments mimic, may not be enough to alter core generic beliefs about gender associations on which attitudes rest, no matter how realistic the treatments or potent the dosage (Tavits et al. 2024). That is, we do not find evidence that the type of normalized counter-stereotypical information that we are interested in and is of interest to policymakers and policy entrepreneurs increase equitable attitudes. Instead, what might be needed is an active and experiential engagement with counter-stereotypical gender roles. For example, it is possible that adopting counter-stereotypical language and images (similar to those used in our treatments) in a wide variety of everyday contexts (e.g., books, media) that involve constant and active engagement will have the ability to reshape generic core beliefs about gender and nudge public attitudes in more gender- and LGBTQ-equitable directions.[29] It is also possible that, as Diekman and Eagly (1999) argue, people are implicit role theorists whose stereotypes change in response to sustained changes in gender roles in society over years and decades. In other words, simply exposing people to normalized counter-stereotypes may not be enough. Long-term, experiential engagement with normalized counter-stereotypies may be needed.

5.5 A Path Forward for Future Research?

In this section, we discuss more specifically potential research ideas for the future. One option might be to devise an observational study to examine a more

---

[29] Prior studies use the trait perception questions of the sort we used in the context of assessing specific candidates (e.g., Bauer 2017; 2020; Huddy and Terkildsen 1993). Therefore, they are used differently from how we use it – to measure core beliefs about women and men generally. Given our null findings, as we elaborate in the next section, we speculate that constant and experiential engagement with normalized counter-stereotypes in everyday life may be necessary to change such fundamental beliefs.

prolonged situation in which people face counter-stereotypical information about gender roles. In line with our first experiment, one could, for example, focus on the domain of religion, which is traditionally very male-dominant. We saw from the tests associated with Study 1 that the gender stereotype of God is strongly male. Moreover, because clergy is dominated by men in most major denominations, a larger presence of female leaders in church exposes individuals to a counter-stereotypical gender role in a normalized way. This would offer a context where we can examine whether such exposure shapes people's attitudes toward gender equality and LGBTQ tolerance. A religious context would be more advantageous than a political one also because female clergy are likely to have longer tenure than female politicians and the political domain is highly endogenous due to voting.

This would require studying a context with an established and dominant church with a high affiliation rate to maximize the chances that people are exposed to its leaders. The Church of England (CoE) in the UK would be one such possibility. The CoE ordained female priests for the first time in 1994, after the decision of the General Synod (the legislature of the Church) in 1992. Diocese-level data from 2014, for example, shows that, on average, 16.43 percent posts were held by women, with the highest share being about 50 percent. This allows for quite a bit of variance in real-world exposure to women in counter-stereotypical roles, the effects of which could be explored cross-sectionally and over time with diocese-level survey data.

Of course, as with any observational data, one might be concerned that local-level attitudes about gender might influence the percentage of female clergy in the diocese. If more female clergy are assigned in dioceses that have high levels of equitable attitudes about women and sexual minorities (and, conversely, if more male clergy are assigned in places that are hostile to women and sexual minorities), then examining the effect of female clergy presence on people's attitudes is looking at the wrong causal order.

To overcome the challenge of causal inference, one could adopt field experimental designs that would allow randomizing one's long-term exposure to counter-stereotypical roles. This presents its own challenges as implementing such randomizations are not always practical or ethical, and randomizations that happen naturally are rare. That said, and thinking again about nonpolitical contexts, an increasing acceptance of women in the military might offer an opportunity (see Dahl et al. 2021), especially if women are randomized to join certain units and not others. Even then, however, challenges continue because this would allow studying the attitudes of a very specialized population only. The same is true for studying other potential policy interventions. For example, a recent study examines whether granting fathers parental leave promotes gender equality attitudes (Tavits et al. 2024). The study explores whether direct exposure to such a social policy intervention, which offers men the opportunity to engage in a counter-stereotypical gender role, has the power to weaken ingrained sexist attitudes. Tavits et al. overcome the challenge of non-random selection by focusing on a reform in Estonia that extended fathers' leave threefold for children born on or after July 1, 2020 and find that direct exposure to the reform promotes more gender-equal attitudes. But the conclusions only extend to the limited group of new mothers and fathers, making it difficult to draw general inferences about the power of counter-stereotypes to reduce attitudinal gender bias. Moreover, their study does not address attitudes about the LGBTQ.

Since we are interested in normalized counter-stereotypes that are part of everyday life, one possible novel approach might be to conduct a project where textbooks that children use in school embed counter-stereotypical gender information in their learning content. This is obviously an ambitious, large-scale, and collaborative project that few researchers will be able to implement, although smaller-scale studies of this kind exist in other disciplines and with respect to outcomes other than attitudes (e.g., Good et al. 2010). Alternatively, an interesting though unconventional way to convey normalized counter-stereotypes is to provide immersive experiences in a counter-stereotypical position through, for example, the use of virtual reality simulations that allow participants to experience different gender roles and identities. Implementing such large-scale creative designs remains beyond the scope of this Element. Nonetheless, the findings of this Element present the direction that future research should take when trying to understand the effects of normalized gender counter-stereotypes on gender-related attitudes. Innovative research designs can help shed light on the complex and dynamic ways in which counter-stereotypes about gender can impact individuals' attitudes and behaviors, and ultimately contribute to a more equitable and just society.

6 Conclusion

Drawing insights from social psychology and the gender and politics literature, we tested whether exposure to gender counter-stereotypes increases the equitability of gender-related attitudes. Contrary to theoretical expectations and assumptions in real-life counter-stereotype campaigns, none of our experiments provide evidence that undermining gender-role stereotypes increases gender- and LGBTQ-equitable attitudes. If anything, there is some, though very limited, evidence that counter-stereotypical information can reduce equitable attitudes. These results are important given the strong theoretical backing for the original expectation as well as the real-life relevance of the treatments that we used.

Note that our null findings do not imply that (a) stereotypes are an unimportant source of bias or (b) increasing women's presence in male-dominant positions will not break barriers to female empowerment (Barnes and Burchard 2013; Krook 2010; Matland 1994; O'Brien and Rickne 2016). Our results imply, however, that the role of counter-stereotypes in making gains with respect to the fundamental attitudes people have about women are nuanced and complex. We know from prior research that stereotypes are resilient and our experimental studies further suggest that brief and passive exposure to specific counter-stereotypical examples, no matter how realistic or strong, may not be enough to alter attitudes. Instead, one might need to combine strong, realistic counter-stereotypes (as we did in our experiments) with chronic, active, and experiential exposure to produce effects – something that policymakers and future studies should explore. For example, a field experiment using textbooks with gender counter-stereotypical content to engage students over the long term, or providing immersive experience in a counter-stereotypical role, would be the types of interventions that bring the treatments we used in this Element to a long-term, experiential context. Building on our findings in this manner would have high policy relevance in the context of ongoing attempts to promote gender and LGBTQ equity. While we do not mean to say that brief and passive exposure to counter-stereotypes in real life are fruitless, they do not easily contribute to equitable attitudes.

Moreover, our findings contribute significantly to different sets of literatures. In the field of gender and politics, existing research on gender equality has acknowledged the potential importance of female role models and social norms about gender roles on equitable outcomes (Barnes and Burchard 2013; Beaman et al. 2012; O'Brien and Rickne 2016), and has explored the role of gender stereotypes in political evaluations (Bauer 2015; Beaman et al. 2009; Dolan 2014; Holman et al. 2016; Sanbonmatsu 2002). Increases in the political representation of women in democracies around the world are indeed part of the process of normalizing gender counter-stereotypes. The research we advance in this Element adds to this body of work by focusing specifically on gender-role counter-stereotypes and exploring whether and how these could be used to undermine inequitable attitudes in the gender domain. In doing so, our work connects studies of stereotypes in social psychology and political science.

Furthermore, it remains to be seen whether our findings are confined to the realm of gender or extend to other domains. Our findings are rather consistent with previous research on racial stereotypes and attitudes (Lai et al. 2014), which has mainly focused on implicit attitudes but find that when it comes to explicit attitudes, racial counter-stereotypes do not consistently reduce racial bias. Nonetheless, it may be that equalizing attitudes by undermining stereotypes is more difficult in the gender domain than in other domains. This is reflected in the variety of ways in which gender attitudes have been measured in previous research, pointing to the multidimensional, nuanced nature of gender attitudes (Schaffner 2022a). Moreover, gender stereotypes may be less (not more) malleable because people unavoidably have intimate, kinship relations with the opposite sex, unlike in the racial domain (Fiske and Stevens 1993). Attitudes about the LGBTQ are also influenced by social contact, i.e., having a close friend or family member who is gay, lesbian, or transgender (Becker 2012; Flores 2015; Lewis 2011; Norton and Herek 2013). In addition, socialization during early stages of one's life is likely to shape attitudes about gender equality and LGBTQ issues, hence making them more resistant to change. Healy and Malhotra (2013) find that having female siblings leads to more conservative political views among young men, the mechanism being that families with (more) female children tend to reinforce traditional gender roles in the house. More generally, sociological work demonstrates that gender roles experienced in childhood has long-term effects on a variety of aspects of life in adulthood (e.g., Lindsey 1997; West and Zimmerman 1987). It is therefore important to continue exploring the power and limits of counter-stereotypes to undermine prejudice more broadly.

Better understanding the power and limits of counter-stereotypes also contributes to the literature on attitudes toward LGBTQ individuals. The extant literature has examined various predictors of LGBTQ attitudes, such as language, LGBTQ policies, and exposure. (Abou-Chadi and Finnigan 2019; Andersen and Fetner 2008; Ayoub and Garretson 2017; Flores et al. 2018; Lewis et al. 2017; Tavits and Pérez 2019). Recent work has also specifically investigated the effects of interpersonal conversation on transphobia (Broockman and Kalla 2016; Kalla and Broockman 2020). Most relevantly for this Element, some have focused on the influence of gender attitudes/ stereotypes (Tavits and Pérez 2019) or the effects of related constructs like (gender) norms (Ayoub and Garretson 2017; Flores et al. 2018). Hence, the connections between the literatures on gender and the LGBTQ community deserve greater attention. Yet there has been a lack of studies that examine whether directly countering gender stereotypes can make attitudes toward LGBTQ individuals more tolerant and equitable – the gap this Element and the proposed research agenda start to fill. This is an important contribution considering the gender-stereotypical foundations of LGBTQ attitudes that have been identified in research outside of political science (Blashill and Powlishta 2009; Lehavot and Lambert 2007; Whitehead 2014).

In addition, our work speaks to the literature on the effects of social norms on attitudes and group stereotypes. Institutional decisions about political issues set the social norm and give legitimacy to a particular position on the issue. Previous work has therefore explored whether institutional decisions shape public opinion on issues ranging from LGBTQ rights to abortion (e.g., Jung and Tavits 2021a; Matthews 2005; Tankard and Paluck 2017; Thompson 2022). There is mixed evidence on this front. On the one hand, according to Thompson (2022), exposure to the 2020 US Supreme Court ruling against discrimination based on sexual orientation or gender identity (*Bostock v. Clayton County*) increased favorability toward sexual and gender minorities. Matthews (2005) attributes rapid increase in support for gay marriage in Canada to the framing and persuasive effects of equal-rights-based, legal recognition that started off with the landmark Supreme Court decision, *M. v. H*, which involved a dispute about spousal support after the break-up of a same-sex relationship. The decision affirmed that lack of legal recognition of same-sex relationships counts as unreasonable limit on equality protected by the Canadian Charter of Rights and Freedoms. But according to Tankard and Paluck (2017), the Supreme Court ruling in favor of same-sex marriage (*Obergefell v. Hodges*) did not consistently increase favorable attitudes about that issue. Similarly, Jung and Tavits (2021a) find that the 2018 abortion referendum in Ireland (whose outcome was in favor of repealing the country's constitutional ban on abortion) did not consistently increase favorable attitudes about abortion. However, all these studies do find that these institutional and informational interventions successfully encourage people to update their perception of the social norm on the issue. This Element contributes to this line of work by speaking to the norm-changing effects of embedding counter-stereotypes in everyday life.

Appendix

A1 Survey Instruments for Studies 2–5

In this section, we present the treatments for Studies 2–5. The outcome questions for Studies 2–5 are the same, so we present them only once under Study 2. Note that Study 5 combines the treatments used in Studies 1–3, so we do not present them again. See Section 3 for information on Study 1.

As briefly noted in Section 3, we chose picture pairs that we deem are parallel except for gender. We also purposefully chose pictures of individuals who are not widely known, so that our US-based respondents were unlikely to recognize any of them. In Study 2, we did not use pictures of well-known presidents because we did not want to prime the associations that survey respondents might have about those figures and thus interfere with our goal of understanding the effect of generalized gender counter-stereotypes. Hence, as shown later, we chose a picture of the women presidents of the three Eastern European countries (Croatia, Estonia, Lithuania) from 2017 standing next to each other and a picture of the three male presidents of Bosnia and Herzegovina from 2014 to 2018 standing next to each other.[1] They are formal group pictures with a similar background. We omit the presentation of pictures used in Studies 3 and 4 because of missing copyright information. But we describe the pictures here, and further information is available upon request. For Study 3, we found a generic picture of a male housekeeper and a generic picture of a female housekeeper, both of which are very commonly used at various sites across the internet. The pictures have the same color scheme. The two housekeepers are smiling, wearing a white shirt and an apron, holding similar cleaning equipment, and facing in the same direction. In Study 4, we used a picture of a male singer and a picture of a female singer, both capturing the moment they are singing into a microphone. The pictures are in gray scale and are bust shots from a side angle, both singers facing to the right. The singers in the pictures are not well-known individuals that survey respondents would recognize. For these reasons, while we did not pre-test the pictures before running the experiments, we are confident that the picture pairs are isolating gender differences. All of the pictures used in the experiments are available on the internet.

---

[1] Survey respondents did not see the copyright information to the right of the images.

[Study 2]

Female President Treatment

Here is how encyclopedias define a president. Please read this information carefully and answer the question at the bottom to continue with the survey.

(© Robertas Dačkus)

The president is the officer in whom the chief executive power of a nation is vested. Her power varies from country to country. In the U.S., Africa, and Latin America, she is charged with great powers and responsibilities. But she is relatively weak and largely ceremonial in Europe and in many countries where the prime minister functions as the chief executive officer.

Source: *Encyclopedia Britannica*

According to the description, what are the characteristics of a president?

• She is the officer in whom the chief executive power of a nation is vested.

• Her power varies across countries.

• She has great powers and responsibilities in the U.S., Africa, and Latin America.

• All of the above.

Male President Treatment

Here is how encyclopedias define a president. Please read this information carefully and answer the question at the bottom to continue with the survey.

(Courtesy of The Press Office of The Presidency of Bosnia and Herzegovina)

The president is the officer in whom the chief executive power of a nation is vested. His power varies from country to country. In the U.S., Africa, and Latin America, he is charged with great powers and responsibilities. But he is relatively weak and largely ceremonial in Europe and in many countries where the prime minister functions as the chief executive officer.

Source: *Encyclopedia Britannica*

According to the description, what are the characteristics of a president?
- He is the officer in whom the chief executive power of a nation is vested.
- His power varies across countries.
- He has great powers and responsibilities in the U.S., Africa, and Latin America.
- All of the above.

Next, we would like to ask for your opinion on some social issues. Please indicate the degree to which you agree or disagree with the following statements:

- Wives should not have to do more housework than husbands do.
- Political parties should do more to encourage qualified women to run for political office.
- On the whole, men make better political leaders than women do.
- Homosexual couples should have the right to marry one another.
- Our society has not gone far enough in accepting people who are transgender.
- Someone can be a man or a woman even if that is different from the sex they were assigned at birth.

(Answer options for each of the statements are: Strongly agree, Somewhat agree, Somewhat disagree, Strongly disagree.)

[Study 3]

Male Housekeeper Treatment
Here is how career consultants define a housekeeper. Please read this information carefully and answer the question at the bottom to continue with the survey.

[Picture of male housekeeper here]

A housekeeper performs essential tasks like emptying our office trash cans at night, as well as mopping floors, making beds and polishing furniture in our hotel rooms. In general, he dusts around, soaps up, suds down and mops away our messes, helping keep our lives running smoothly (and hygienically). He works in hotels, motels, or private households.

Source: *U.S. News and World Report*

According to the description, what are the characteristics of a housekeeper?
- He performs essential cleaning tasks.
- He helps our lives run smoothly.
- He works in hotels, motels, or private households.
- All of the above.

Female Housekeeper Treatment
Here is how career consultants define a housekeeper. Please read this information carefully and answer the question at the bottom to continue with the survey.

[Picture of female housekeeper here]

A housekeeper performs essential tasks like emptying our office trash cans at night, as well as mopping floors, making beds and polishing furniture in our hotel rooms. In general, she dusts around, soaps up, suds down and mops away our messes, helping keep our lives running smoothly (and hygienically). She works in hotels, motels, or private households.

Source: *U.S. News and World Report*

According to the description, what are the characteristics of a housekeeper?
- She performs essential cleaning tasks.
- She helps our lives run smoothly.
- She works in hotels, motels, or private households.
- All of the above.

[Study 4]

Female Singer Treatment
Here is how career consultants define a singer. Please read this information carefully and answer the question at the bottom to continue with the survey.

[Picture of female singer here]

A singer sings the main vocal line of a track. She is the main focus of the performance. She records albums of songs that she has written or that has been written for her by a production team. Her days are spent in studio, on tour, and practicing vocal, instrumental or dance skills.

Source: CareersInMusic.com

According to the description, what are the characteristics of a singer?
- She sings the main vocal line of a track.
- She is the main focus of the performance.
- She records albums of songs.
- All of the above.

Male Singer Treatment
Here is how career consultants define a singer. Please read this information carefully and answer the question at the bottom to continue with the survey.

[Picture of male singer here]

A singer sings the main vocal line of a track. He is the main focus of the performance. He records albums of songs that he has written or that has been written for her by a production team. His days are spent in studio, on tour, and practicing vocal, instrumental or dance skills.

Source: CareersInMusic.com

According to the description, what are the characteristics of a singer?
- He sings the main vocal line of a track.
- He is the main focus of the performance.
- He records albums of songs.
- All of the above.

A2 Balance and Randomization Tests

Tables A1–A5 show that there is balance between experimental arms for Studies 1–5. Table A6 show similar results using randomization checks for each study.

Table A1 Balance tests (study 1).

	Range	Male God	Female God	t-test	Chi-square test
Female	[0,1]	0.52	0.51	t = 0.34	
Age	[1.9,9.9]	5.58	5.49	t = 1.18	
Education	[3,15]	11.35	11.32	t = 0.46	
Household income	[1,16]	7.04	6.97	t = 0.42	
Non-White	[0,1]	0.84	0.83	t = 0.34	
Ideology	[1,7]	4.13	4.09	t = 0.57	
Region					$X^2(3) = 2.97$

Table A2 Balance tests (study 2).

	Range	Male president	Female president	t-test	Chi-square test
Female	[0,1]	0.53	0.49	t = 1.07	
Age	[1.8,9.7]	4.46	4.42	t = 0.38	
Education	[1,11]	4.47	4.57	t = −0.89	
Household income	[1,24]	8.88	8.46	t = 1.04	
Non-White	[0,1]	0.26	0.29	t = −0.99	
Ideology	[1,7]	3.88	3.82	t = 0.48	
Region					$X^2(3) = 4.08$

Table A3 Balance tests (study 3).

	Range	Female housekeeper	Male housekeeper	t-test	Chi-square test
Female	[0,1]	0.51	0.51	t = −0.12	
Age	[1.8,9.0]	4.68	4.44	t = 2.59	
Education	[1,11]	4.54	4.44	t = −0.87	
Household income	[1,24]	8.94	9.08	t = −0.34	
Non-White	[0,1]	0.27	0.24	t = 1.00	
Ideology	[1,7]	3.83	3.74	t = 0.66	
Region					$X^2(3) = 1.09$

Table A4 Balance tests (study 4).

	Range	Female singer	Male singer	t-test	Chi-square test
Female	[0,1]	0.53	0.49	t = 1.42	
Age	[1.8,8.6]	4.52	4.48	t = 0.45	
Education	[1,9]	4.33	4.53	t = −1.88	
Household income	[1,24]	8.34	9.09	t = −1.95	
Non-White	[0,1]	0.27	0.26	t = 0.52	
Ideology	[1,7]	3.87	3.75	t = 0.95	
Region					$X^2(3) = 4.06$

Table A5 Balance tests (study 5).

	Range	Stereotype	Counter-stereotype	t-test	Chi-square test
Female	[0,1]	0.51	0.56	t = −1.71	
Age	[1.8,8.5]	3.36	3.34	t = 0.33	
Education	[1,7]	4.23	4.21	t = 0.23	
Household income	[1,13]	7.42	7.18	t = 1.15	
Non-White	[0,1]	0.31	0.29	t = 0.99	
Partisanship					$X^2(3) = 2.31$
Region					$X^2(3) = 4.29$

Table A6 Randomization checks.

	Study 1	Study 2	Study 3	Study 4	Study 5
Female	−0.08	−0.13	0.03	−0.14	0.18
	(0.09)	(0.12)	(0.12)	(0.12)	(0.12)
Age	−0.04	−0.00	−0.10*	−0.01	−0.03
	(0.03)	(0.04)	(0.04)	(0.04)	(0.05)
Income	−0.01	−0.01	0.00	0.01	−0.01
	(0.01)	(0.01)	(0.01)	(0.01)	(0.02)
Education	−0.02	0.03	−0.03	0.04	0.01
	(0.03)	(0.03)	(0.03)	(0.03)	(0.05)
Non-White	0.12	0.18	−0.24	−0.07	−0.16
	(0.13)	(0.15)	(0.15)	(0.14)	(0.13)
Ideology	−0.02	−0.00	−0.02	−0.03	
	(0.03)	(0.03)	(0.03)	(0.03)	
Independent					−0.08
					(0.14)
Republican					−0.08
					(0.19)
Something else					0.26
					(0.24)
Northeast	0.21	−0.41*	−0.09	0.01	−0.07
	(0.15)	(0.19)	(0.19)	(0.19)	(0.19)
South	0.02	−0.17	−0.17	−0.11	0.24
	(0.12)	(0.16)	(0.17)	(0.17)	(0.16)
West	−0.02	−0.21	−0.20	−0.28	0.15
	(0.13)	(0.18)	(0.19)	(0.19)	(0.17)
Intercept	0.53	0.18	0.75*	0.13	−0.03
	(0.39)	(0.29)	(0.29)	(0.28)	(0.29)
Log Likelihood	−1281.24	−786.28	−784.13	−787.85	−824.09
Num. obs.	1855	1141	1139	1144	1197

Note: *p < 0.05. Study 1: $Prob(X^2(9) > 8.20) = 0.51$. Study 2: $Prob(X^2(9) > 8.18) = 0.42$. Study 3: $Prob(X^2(9) > 10.68) = 0.30$. Study 4: $Prob(X^2(9) > 10.10) = 0.34$. Study 5: Prob $(X^2(11) > 11.22) = 0.43$.

A3 Robustness Tests for Studies 1–3 and 5

Figures A1–A4 show the results of additional analyses for Studies 1–3 and 5, respectively. All analyses use single-item outcome questions.

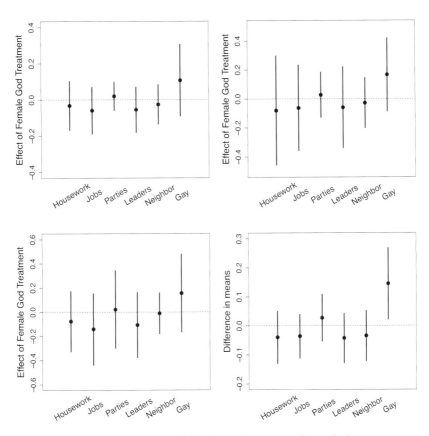

Figure A1 Effect of female god treatment in study 1.

Note: Black circles show coefficient estimates of *Female God* for each single-question outcome variable. Black lines show 95 percent confidence intervals. The top-left panel is OLS with sociodemographic controls; the top-right panel is ordinal logit without controls; the bottom-left panel is ordinal logit with controls; the bottom-right panel is t-test without false discovery rate correction.

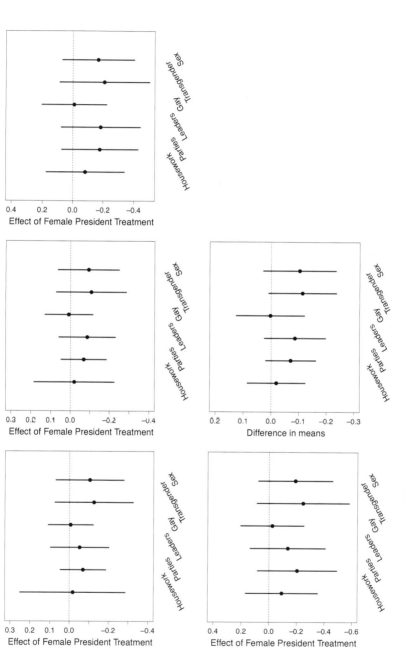

Figure A2 Effect of female president treatment in study 2.

Note: Black circles show coefficient estimates of *Female president* for each single-question outcome variable. Black lines show 95 percent confidence intervals. The first panel is OLS with sociodemographic controls; the second panel is OLS with unbalanced covariates; the third panel is ordinal logit without controls; the fourth panel is ordinal logit with sociodemographic controls; the last panel is t-test without false discovery rate correction.

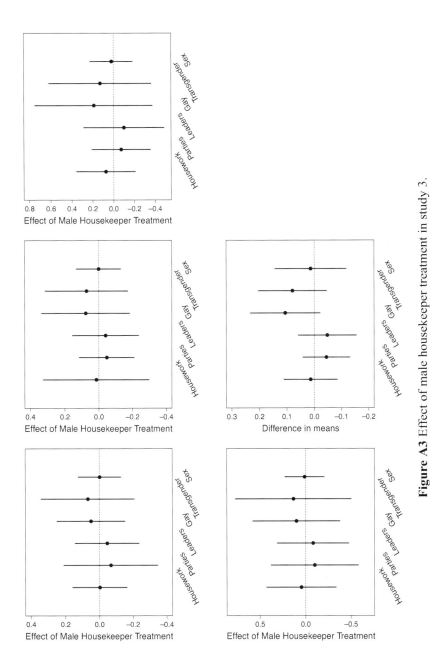

Figure A3 Effect of male housekeeper treatment in study 3.

Note: Black circles show coefficient estimates of *Male housekeeper* for each single-question outcome variable. Black lines show 95 percent confidence intervals. The first panel is OLS with sociodemographic controls; the second panel is OLS with unbalanced covariates; the third panel is ordinal logit without controls; the fourth panel is ordinal logit with sociodemographic controls; the last panel is t-test without false discovery rate correction.

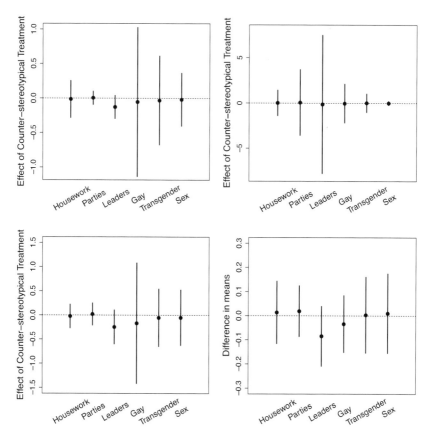

Figure A4 Effect of counter-stereotype treatment in study 5.

Note: Black circles show coefficient estimates of counter-stereotypical treatment for each single-question outcome variable. Black lines show 95 percent confidence intervals. The first panel is OLS with sociodemographic controls; the second panel is ordinal logit without controls; the third panel is ordinal logit with sociodemographic controls; the fourth panel is t-test without false discovery rate correction.

A4 Interaction Analyses between Treatment and Gender

Figures A5–A8 show interaction effects between counter-stereotype treatment and respondent gender using the single-question outcomes in Studies 1–3 and 5, respectively.

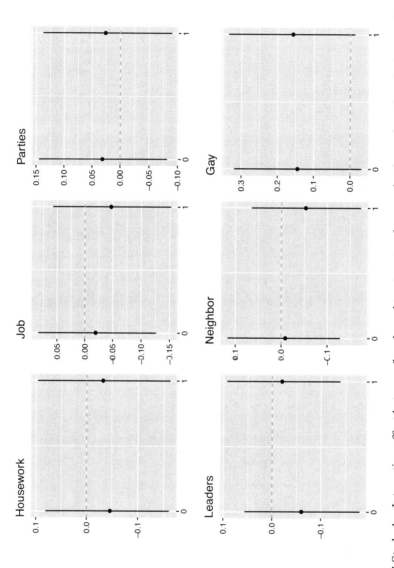

Figure A5 Study 1 – Interaction effect between female god treatment and respondent's gender using single-question outcomes.

Note: Linear regression models. The horizontal axes indicate gender ("0": female, "1": male).

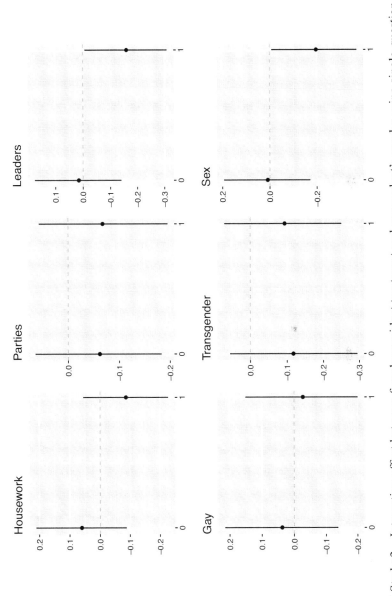

Figure A6 Study 2 – Interaction effect between female president treatment and respondent's gender using single-question outcomes.

Note: Linear regression models. The horizontal axes indicate gender ("0": male, "1": female).

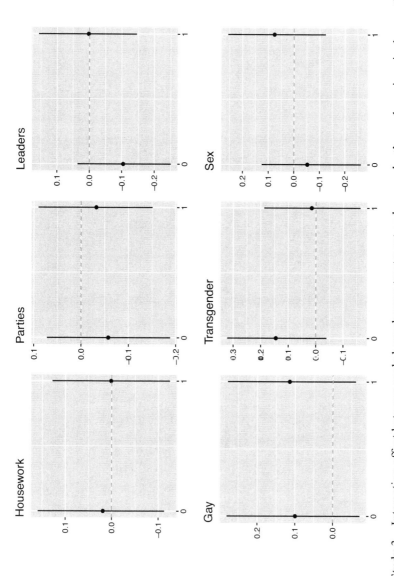

Figure A7 Study 3 – Interaction effect between male housekeeper treatment and respondent's gender using single-question outcomes.
Note: Linear regression models. The horizontal axes indicate gender ("0": male, "1": female).

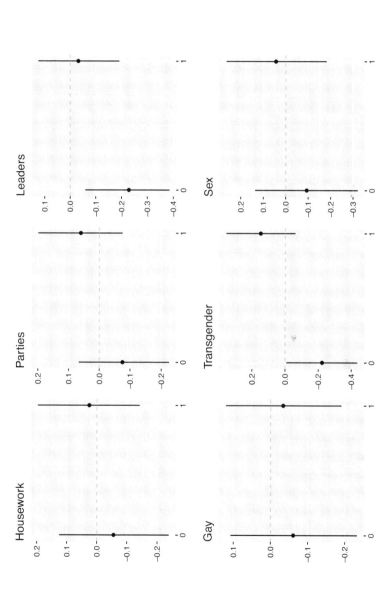

Figure A8 Study 5 – Interaction effect between counter-stereotype treatment and respondent's gender using single-question outcomes.

Note: Linear regression models. The horizontal axes indicate gender ("0": male, "1": female).

A5 Interaction Analyses between Treatment and Education

Figures A9–A12 show interaction effects between counter-stereotype treatment and respondent's education level using the single-question outcomes in Studies 1–3 and 5, respectively.

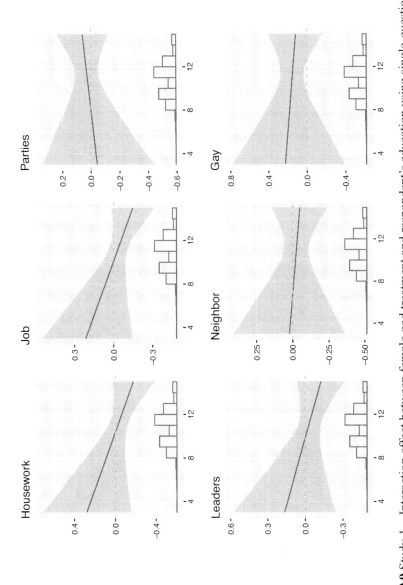

Figure A9 Study 1 – Interaction effect between female god treatment and respondent's education using single-question outcomes.

Note: Linear regression models. Higher values on the horizontal axis indicate higher education levels.

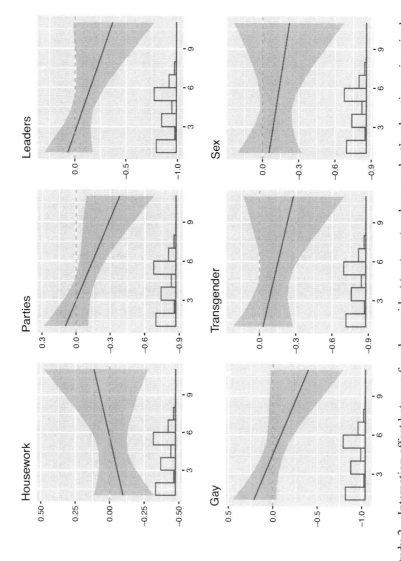

Figure A10 Study 2 – Interaction effect between female president treatment and respondent's education using single-question outcomes.

Note: Linear regression models. Higher values on the horizontal axis indicate higher education levels.

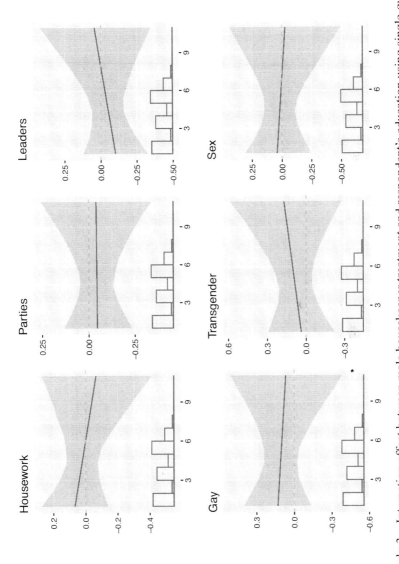

Figure A11 Study 3 – Interaction effect between male housekeeper treatment and respondent's education using single-question outcomes.

Note: Linear regression models. Higher values on the horizontal axis indicate higher education levels.

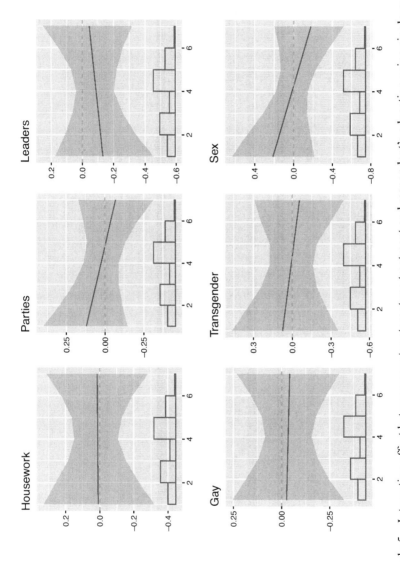

Figure A12 Study 5 – Interaction effect between counter-stereotype treatment and respondent's education using single-question outcomes.

Note: Linear regression models. Higher values on the horizontal axis indicate higher education levels.

A6 Interaction Analyses between Treatment and Ideology

Figures A13–A15 show interaction effects between counter-stereotype treatment and respondent ideology using the single-question outcomes in Studies 1, 2, and 3, respectively. We do not include Study 5 because it did not include a good measure of ideology.

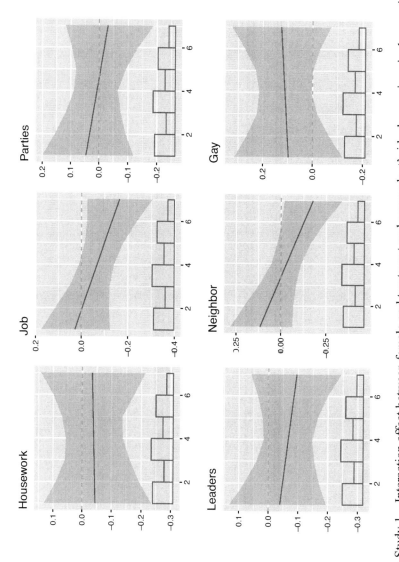

Figure A13 Study 1 – Interaction effect between female god treatment and respondent's ideology using single-question outcomes.

Note: Linear regression models. Higher values on the horizontal axes indicate more conservative attitudes.

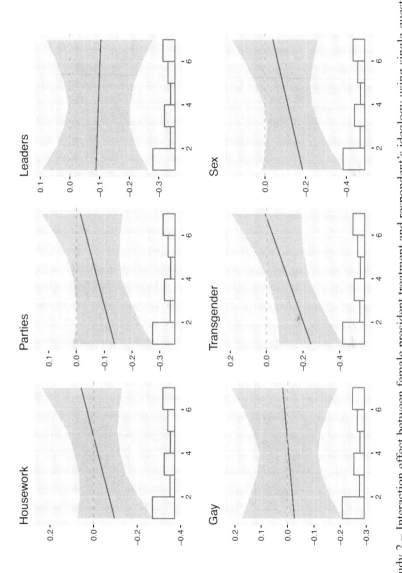

Figure A14 Study 2 — Interaction effect between female president treatment and respondent's ideology using single-question outcomes.

Note: Linear regression models. Higher values on the horizontal axes indicate more conservative attitudes.

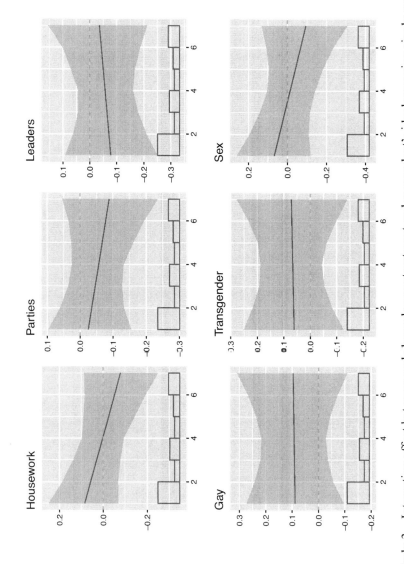

Figure A15 Study 3 – Interaction effect between male housekeeper treatment and respondent's ideology using single-question outcomes.

Note: Linear regression models. Higher values on the horizontal axes indicate more conservative attitudes.

A7 Ceiling Effects

Figures A16–A19 show the distributions of the single-item outcome variables for Studies 1–3 and 5, respectively. Since there is sufficient variation in the data, the distributions show that ceiling effects are unlikely why we observe overall null effects of counter-stereotype treatments.

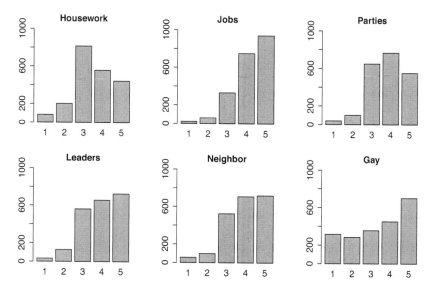

Figure A16 Distributions of single-question outcomes in study 1.

Note: Higher values on the horizontal axes indicate more liberal attitudes.

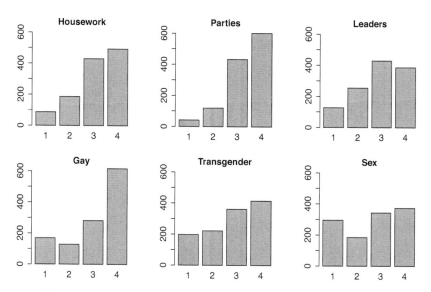

Figure A17 Distributions of single-question outcomes in study 2.

Note: Higher values on the horizontal axes indicate more liberal attitudes.

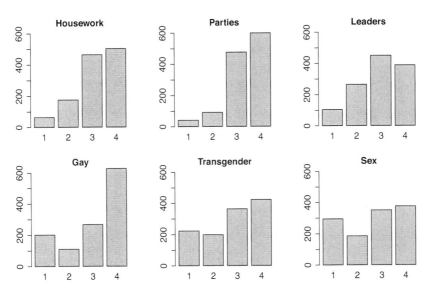

Figure A18 Distributions of single-question outcomes in study 3.

Note: Higher values on the horizontal axes indicate more liberal attitudes.

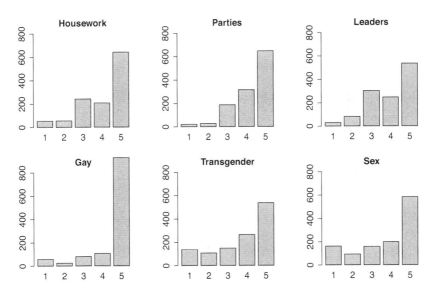

Figure A19 Distributions of single-question outcomes in study 5.

Note: Higher values on the horizontal axes indicate more liberal attitudes.

References

Abou-Chadi, Tarik and Ryan Finnigan. 2019. "Rights for Same-Sex Couples and Public Attitudes Toward Gays and Lesbians in Europe." *Comparative Political Studies* 52(6): 868–895.

Allport, Gordon W. 1954. *The Nature of Prejudice*. Reading, MA: Addison-Wesley.

Andersen, Robert and Tina Fetner. 2008. "Economic Inequality and Intolerance: Attitudes toward Homosexuality in 35 Democracies." *American Journal of Political Science* 52(4): 942–958.

Ayoub, Phillip M. and Jeremiah Garretson. 2017. "Getting the Message Out: Media Context and Global Changes in Attitudes toward Homosexuality." *Comparative Political Studies* 50(8): 1055–1085.

Bakker, Bert N., David Nicolas Hopmann and Mikael Persson. 2015. "Personality Traits and Party Identification Over Time." *European Journal of Political Research* 54: 197–215.

Barnes, Tiffany D. and Stephanie M. Burchard. 2013. "'Engendering' Politics: The Impact of Descriptive Representation on Women's Political Engagement in Sub-Saharan Africa." *Comparative Political Studies* 46(7): 767–790.

Barnes, Tiffany D. and Diana Z. O'Brien. 2018. "Defending the Realm: The Appointment of Female Defense Ministers Worldwide." *American Journal of Political Science* 62(2): 355–368.

Bauer, Nichole M. 2015. "Emotional, Sensitive, and Unfit for Office? Gender Stereotype Activation and Support Female Candidates." *Political Psychology* 36(6): 691–708.

Bauer, Nichole M. 2017. "The Effects of Counterstereotypic Gender Strategies on Candidate Evaluations." *Political Psychology* 38(2): 279–295.

Bauer, Nichole M. 2020. "Running Local: Gender Stereotyping and Female Candidates in Local Elections." *Urban Affairs Review* 56(1): 96–123.

Beaman, Lori, Esther Duflo, Rohini Pande and Petia Topalova. 2012. "Female Leadership Raises Aspirations and Educational Attainment for Girls: A Policy Experiment in India." *Science* 335(6068): 582–586.

Beaman, Lori, Raghabendra Chattopadhyay, Esther Duflo, Rohini Pande and Petia Topalova. 2009. "Powerful Women: Does Exposure Reduce Bias?" *The Quarterly Journal of Economics* 124(4): 1497–1540.

Becker, Amy B. 2012. "Determinants of Public Support for Same-Sex Marriage: Generational Cohorts, Social Contact, and Shifting Attitudes." *International Journal of Public Opinion Research* 24(4): 524–533.

Becker, Amy B. and Philip Edward Jones. 2021. "Experience with Discrimination, Perceptions of Difference, and the Importance of Gender Conformity on Support for Transgender Rights." *Politics, Groups, and Identities* 9(5): 1051–1067.

Bem, Sandra L. 1981. "Gender Schema Theory: A Cognitive Account of Sex Typing." *Psychological Review* 88(4): 354–364.

Bernhard, Rachel. 2021. "Wearing the Pants(suit)? Gendered Leadership Styles, Partisanship, and Candidate Evaluation in the 2016 U.S. Election." *Politics & Gender* 18(2): 513–545.

Blair, Irene V., Jennifer E. Ma and Alison P. Lenton. 2001. "Imagining Stereotypes Away: The Moderation of Implicit Stereotypes through Mental Imagery." *Journal of Personality and Social Psychology* 81(5): 828–841.

Blashill, Aaron J. and Kimberly K. Powlishta. 2009. "Gay Stereotypes: The Use of Sexual Orientation as a Cue for Gender-Related Attributes." *Sex Roles* 61 (11–12): 783–793.

Bodenhausen, Galen V., Andrew R. Todd and Jennifer A. Richeson. 2009. "Controlling Prejudice and Stereotyping: Antecedents, Mechanisms, and Contexts." In *Handbook of Prejudice, Stereotyping, and Discrimination*, ed. Todd D. Nelson. New York: Psychology Press, pp. 111–135.

Boysen, Guy A. and David L. Vogel. 2007. "Biased Assimilation and Attitude Polarization in Response to Learning about Biological Explanations of Homosexuality." *Sex Roles* 57: 755–762.

Brooks, Deborah Jordan. 2011. "Testing the Double Standard for Candidate Emotionality: Voter Reactions to the Tears and Anger of Male and Female Politicians." *Journal of Politics* 73(2): 597–615.

Brooks, Deborah Jordan. 2013. *He Runs, She Runs: Why Gender Stereotypes Do Not Harm Women Candidates*. Princeton: Princeton University Press.

Broockman, David and Joshua Kalla. 2016. "Durably Reducing Transphobia: A Field Experiment on Door-To-Door Canvassing." *Science* 352(6282): 220–224.

Burgess, Diana and Eugene Borgida. 1999. "Who Women Are, Who Women Should Be: Descriptive and Prescriptive Gender Stereotyping in Sex Discrimination." *Psychology, Public Policy, and Law* 5(3): 665–692.

Carruthers, Peter. 2018. "Implicit Versus Explicit Attitudes: Differing Manifestations of the Same Representational Structures?" *Review of Philosophy and Psychology* 9(1): 51–72.

Cassese, Erin C. and Tiffany D. Barnes. 2019. "Reconciling Sexism and Women's Support for Republican Candidates: A Look at Gender, Class, and Whiteness in the 2012 and 2016 Presidential Races." *Political Behavior* 41: 677–700.

Cassese, Erin C. and Mirya R. Holman. 2018. "Party and Gender Stereotypes in Campaign Attacks." *Political Behavior* 40: 785–807.

Clifford, Scott and Jennifer Jerit. 2015. "Do Attempts to Improve Respondent Attention Increase Social Desirability Bias?" *Public Opinion Quarterly* 79(3): 790–802.

Cohen, Jacob. 1988. *Statistical Power Analysis for the Behavioral Sciences*. 2 ed. New York: Academic Press.

Costa, Mia. 2021. "He Said, She Said: The Gender Double Bind in Legislator–Constituent Communication." *Politics & Gender* 17: 528–551.

Costa, Mia and Isabel Wallace. 2021. "More Women Candidates: The Effects of Increased Women's Presence on Political Ambition, Efficacy, and Vote Choice." *American Politics Research* 49(4): 368–380.

Dahl, Gordon B., Andreas Kotsadam, and Dan-Olof Rooth. 2021. "Does Integration Change Gender Attitudes? The Effect of Randomly Assigning Women to Traditionally Male Teams." *Quarterly Journal of Economics* 136(2): 987–1030.

Damann, Taylor, Jeremy Siow, and Margit Tavits. 2023. "Persistence of Gender Biases in Europe." *Proceedings of the National Academy of Sciences* 120 (12): e2213266120. https://doi.org/10.1073/pnas.221326612.

Dasgupta, Nilanjana and Shaki Asgari. 2004. "Seeing Is Believing: Exposure to Counter Stereotypic Women Leaders and Its Effect on the Malleability of Automatic Gender Stereotyping." *Journal of Experimental Social Psychology* 40: 642–658.

Dasgupta, Nilanjana and Anthony G. Greenwald. 2001. "On the Malleability of Automatic Attitudes: Combating Automatic Prejudice with Images of Admired and Disliked Individuals." *Journal of Personality and Social Psychology* 81(5): 800–814.

Deckman, Melissa and Erin Cassese. 2021. "Gendered Nationalism and the 2016 US Presidential Election: How Party, Class, and Beliefs about Masculinity Shaped Voting Behavior." *Politics & Gender* 17: 277–300.

Diekman, Amanda B. and Alice H. Eagly. 1999. "Stereotypes as Dynamic Constructs: Women and Men of the Past, Present, and Future." *Personality and Social Psychology Bulletin* 26(10): 1171–1188.

Ditonto, Tessa. 2019. "Direct and Indirect Effects of Prejudice: Sexism, Information, and Voting Behavior in Political Campaigns." *Politics, Groups, and Identities* 7(3): 590–609.

Ditonto, Tessa M., Allison J. Hamilton and David P. Redlawsk. 2014. "Gender Stereotypes, Information Search, and Voting Behavior in Political Campaigns." *Political Behavior* 36: 335–358.

Ditonto, Tessa M., Richard R. Lau and David O. Sears. 2013. "AMPing Racial Attitudes: Comparing the Power of Explicit and Implicit Racism Measures in 2008." *Political Psychology* 34(4): 287–510.

Dolan, Kathleen. 2010. "The Impact of Gender Stereotyped Evaluations on Support for Women Candidates." *Political Behavior* 32(1): 69–88.

Dolan, Kathleen. 2014. "Gender Stereotypes, Candidate Evaluations, and Voting for Women Candidates: What Really Matters?" *Political Research Quarterly* 67(1): 96–107.

Eagly, Alice H. and Steven J. Karau. 2002. "Role Congruity Theory of Prejudice toward Female Leaders." *Psychological Review* 109(3): 573–598.

Eagly, Alice H. and Sabine Sczesny. 2009. "Stereotypes About Women, Men, and Leaders: Have Times Changed?" In *The Glass Ceiling in the 21st Century: Understanding Barriers to Gender Equality*, ed. Manuela Barreto, Michelle K. Ryan, & Michael T. Schmitt. Washington, DC: American Psychological Association, pp. 21–47.

Effron, Daniel A., Jessica S. Cameron and Benoît Monin. 2009. "Endorsing Obama Licenses Favoring Whites." *Journal of Experimental Social Psychology* 45: 590–593.

Ellemers, Naomi. 2018. "Gender Stereotypes." *Annual Review of Psychology* 69: 275–298.

Finnegan, Eimear, Alan Garnham and Jane Oakhill. 2015. "Social Consensus Feedback as a Strategy to Overcome Spontaneous Gender Stereotypes." *Discourse Processes* 52(5–6): 434–462.

Finnegan, Eimear, Jane Oakhill and Alan Garnham. 2015. "Counter-Stereotypical Pictures as a Strategy for Overcoming Spontaneous Gender Stereotypes." *Frontiers in Psychology* 6(1291): 1–15.

Fiske, Susan T. 1998. "Stereotyping, Prejudice, and Discrimination." In *The Handbook of Social Psychology*, ed. Daniel T. Gilbert, Susan T. Fiske and Gardner Lindzey. 4 ed. Vol. 1 New York: McGraw-Hill, chapter 25, pp. 357–411.

Fiske, Susan T. and Laura E. Stevens. 1993. "What's So Special About Sex? Gender Stereotyping and Discrimination." In *Gender Issues in Contemporary Society: Applied Social Psychology Annual*, ed. Stuart Oskamp and Mark Costanzo. Newbury Park, CA: Sage, pp. 173–196.

Fiske, Susan T. and Shelley E. Taylor. 2013. *Social Cognition: From Brains to Culture*. London: Sage.

Flores, Andrew R. 2015. "Attitudes toward Transgender Rights: Perceived Knowledge and Secondary Interpersonal Contact." *Politics, Groups, and Identities* 3(3): 398–416.

Flores, Andrew R., Donald P. Haider-Markel, Daniel C. Lewis et al. 2018. "Challenged Expectations: Mere Exposure Effects on Attitudes about Transgender People and Rights." *Political Psychology* 39(1): 197–216.

Gawronski, Bertram and Galen V. Bodenhausen. 2006. "Associative and Propositional Processes in Evaluation: An Integrative Review of Implicit and Explicit Attitude Change." *Psychological Bulletin* 132(5): 692–731.

Georgeac, Oriane and Aneeta Rattan. 2019. "Progress in Women's Representation in Top Leadership Weakens People's Disturbance with Gender Inequality in Other Domains." *Journal of Experimental Psychology: General* 148(8): 1435–1453.

Glick, Peter and Susan T. Fiske. 1997. "Hostile and Benevolent Sexism: Measuring Ambivalent Sexist Attitudes toward Women." *Psychology of Women Quarterly* 21: 119–135.

Glick, Peter, Maria Lameiras, Susan T. Fiske et al. 2004. "Bad but Bold: Ambivalent Attitudes toward Men Predict Gender Inequality in 16 Nations." *Journal of Personality and Social Psychology* 86(5): 713–728.

Goh, Jin X., Judith A. Hall and Robert Rosenthal. 2016. "Mini Meta-Analysis of Your Own Studies: Some Arguments on Why and a Primer on How." *Social and Personality Psychology Compass* 10(10): 535–549.

Good, Jessica J., Julie A. Woodzicka, and Lylan C. Wingfield. 2010. "The Effects of Gender Stereotypic and Counter-Stereotypic Textbook Images on Science Performance." *The Journal of Social Psychology* 150(2): 132–147.

Haider-Markel, Donald P. and Mark Joslyn. 2005. "Attributions and the Regulation of Marriage: Considering the Parallels between Race and Homosexuality." *Political Science and Politics* 38(2): 233–240.

Haider-Markel, Donald P. and Mark Josyln. 2008. "Understanding Beliefs About the Origins of Homosexuality and Subsequent Support for Gay Rights: An Empirical Test of Attribution Theory." *Public Opinion Quarterly* 72(2): 291–310.

Healy, Andrew and Neil Malhotra. 2013. "Childhood Socialization and Political Attitudes: Evidence from a Natural Experiment." *Journal of Politics* 75(4): 1023–1037.

Heilman, Madeline E. 2012. "Gender Stereotypes and Workplace Bias." *Research in Organizational Behavior* 32: 113–135.

Holman, Mirya R., Jennifer L. Merolla and Elizabeth J. Zechmeister. 2011. "Sex, Stereotypes, and Security: A Study of the Effects of Terrorist Threat on Assessments of Female Leadership." *Journal of Women, Politics & Policy* 32: 173–192.

Holman, Mirya R., Jennifer L. Merolla and Elizabeth J. Zechmeister. 2016. "Terrorist Threat, Male Stereotypes, and Candidate Evaluations." *Political Research Quarterly* 69(1): 134–147.

Honderich, Ted. 1995. *The Oxford Companion to Philosophy.* Oxford University Press.

Huddy, Leonie and Nayda Terkildsen. 1993. "Gender Stereotypes and the Perception of Male and Female Candidates." *American Journal of Political Science* 37(1): 119–147.

Hurwitz, Jon and Mark Peffley. 1997. "Public Perceptions of Race and Crime: The Role of Racial Stereotypes." *American Journal of Political Science* 41(2): 375–401.

Inglehart, Ronald and Pippa Norris. 2003. *Rising Tide: Gender Equality and Cultural Change around the World.* Cambridge: Cambridge University Press.

Iversen, Torben and Frances Rosenbluth. 2010. *Women, Work, and Politics: The Political Economy of Gender Inequality.* New Haven: Yale University Press.

Jones, Philip Edward, Paul R. Brewer, Dannagal G. Young, Jennifer L. Lambe, and Lindsay H. Hoffman. 2018. "Explaining Public Opinion Toward Transgender People, Rights, and Candidates." *Public Opinion Quarterly* 82(2): 252–278.

Joslyn, Mark R. and Donald P. Haider-Markel. 2016. "Genetic Attributions, Immutability, and Stereotypical Judgments: An Analysis of Homosexuality." *Social Science Quarterly* 97(2): 376–390.

Joy-Gaba, Jennifer A. and Brian Nosek. 2010. "The Surprisingly Limited Malleability of Implicit Racial Evaluations." *Social Psychology* 41(3): 137–146.

Jung, Jae-Hee and Margit Tavits. 2021a. "Do Referendum Results Change Norm Perceptions and Personal Opinions?" *Electoral Studies* 71: 102307.

Jung, Jae-Hee and Margit Tavits. 2021b. "Valence Attacks Harm the Electoral Performance of the Left but not the Right." *Journal of Politics* 83(1): 277–290.

Kalla, Joshua L. and David E. Broockman. 2020. "Reducing Exclusionary Attitudes through Interpersonal Conversation: Evidence from Three Field Experiments." *American Political Science Review* 114(2): 410–425.

Kite, Mary E. and Kay Deaux. 1987. "Gender Belief Systems: Homosexuality and the Implicit Inversion Theory." *Psychology of Women Quarterly* 11: 83–96.

Koch, Jeffrey W. 2000. "Do Citizens Apply Gender Stereotypes to Infer Candidates' Ideological Orientations?" *Journal of Politics* 62(2): 414–429.

Koenig, Anne M. and Alice H. Eagly. 2014. "Evidence for the Social Role Theory of Stereotype Content: Observations of Groups' Roles Shape Stereotypes." *Journal of Personality and Social Psychology* 107(3): 371–392.

Krook, Mona Lena. 2010. *Quotas for Women in Politics: Gender and Candidate Selection Reform Worldwide*. Oxford: Oxford University Press.

Kunda, Ziva and Kathryn C. Oleson. 1995. "Maintaining Stereotypes in the Face of Disconfirmation: Constructing Grounds for Subtyping Deviants." *Journal of Personality and Social Psychology* 68(4): 565–580.

Kunda, Ziva and Kathryn C. Oleson. 1997. "When Exceptions Prove the Rule: How Extremity of Deviance Determines the Impact of Deviant Examples on Stereotypes." *Journal of Personality and Social Psychology* 72(5): 965–979.

Lai, Calvin K., Maddalena Marini, Steven A. Lehr et al. 2014. "Reducing Implicit Racial Preferences: I. A Comparative Investigation of 17 Interventions." *Journal of Experimental Psychology: General* 143(4): 1765–1785.

Lai, calvin K., Allison L. Skinner, Erin Cooley, et al. 2016. "Reducing Implicit Racial Preferences: Intervention Effectiveness across Time." *Journal of Experimental Psychology: General* 145(8): 1001–1016.

Lehavot, Keren and Alan J. Lambert. 2007. "Toward a Greater Understanding of Antigay Prejudice: On the Role of Sexual Orientation and Gender Role Violation." *Basic and Applied Social Psychology* 29(3): 279–292.

Leicht, Carola, Malgorzata A. Goclowska, Jolien A. Van Breen, Soledad de Lemus, and Georgina Randsley de Moura. 2017. "Counter-stereotypes and Feminism Promote Leadership Aspirations in Highly Identified Women." *Frontiers in Psychology* 8: 883.

Lewis, Daniel C., Andrew R. Flores, Donald P. Haider-Markel et al. 2017. "Degrees of Acceptance: Variation in Public Attitudes toward Segments of the LGBT Community." *Political Research Quarterly* 70(4): 861–875.

Lewis, Gregory B. 2011. "The Friends and Family Plan: Contact with Gays and Support for Gay Rights." *Policy Studies Journal* 39(2): 217–238.

Lindsey, Linda L. 1997. *Gender Roles: A Sociological Perspective*. Upper Saddle River, NJ: Prentice Hall.

Liu, Xuan and Bin Zuo. 2006. "Psychological Mechanism of Maintaining Gender Stereo-types." *Advances in Psychological Science* 3: 456-461.

Madon, Stephanie. 1997. "What Do People Believe About Gay Males? A Study of Stereotype Content and Strength." *Sex Roles* 37: 663–685.

Matland, Richard E. 1994. "Putting Scandinavian Equality to the Test: An Experimental Evaluation of Gender Stereotyping of Political Candidates in a Sample of Norwegian Voters." *British Journal of Political Science* 24(2): 273–292.

Matthews, J. Scott. 2005. "The Political Foundations of Support for Same-Sex Marriage in Canada." *Canadian Journal of Political Science* 38(4): 841–866.

Mo, Cecilia Hyunjung. 2015. "The Consequences of Explicit and Implicit Gender Attitudes and Candidate Quality in the Calculations of Voters." *Political Behavior* 37(2): 357–395.

Mummolo, Jonathan and Erik Peterson. 2018. "Demand Effects in Survey Experiments: An Empirical Assessment." *American Political Science Review* 113(2): 517–529.

Norton, Aaron T. and Gregory M. Herek. 2013. "Heterosexuals' Attitudes toward Transgender People: Findings from a National Probability Sample of U.S. Adults." *Sex Roles* 68: 738–753.

Nosek, Brian A., Frederick L. Smyth, Natarajan Sriram et al. 2009. "National Differences in Gender–Science Stereotypes Predict National Sex Differences in Science and Math Achievement." *Proceedings of the National Academy of Sciences* 106(26): 10593–10597.

O'Brien, Diana Z. and Johanna Rickne. 2016. "Gender Quotas and Women's Political Leadership." *American Political Science Review* 110(1): 112–126.

Olsson, Maria and Sarah E. Martiny. 2018. "Does Exposure to Counterstereotypical Role Models Influence Girls' and Women's Gender Stereotypes and Career Choices? A Review of Social Psychological Research." *Frontiers in Psychology* 9(2264): 1–15.

Operario, Don and Susan T. Fiske. 2004. "Stereotypes: Content, Structures, Processes, and Context." In *Social Cognition*, ed. M. B. Brewer and M. Hewstone. Malden: Blackwell, pp. 120–141.

Oswald, Frederick L., Gregory Mitchell, Hart Blanton, James Jaccard and Philip E. Tetlock. 2013. "Predicting Ethnic and Racial Discrimination: A Meta-Analysis of IAT Criterion Studies." *Journal of Personality and Social Psychology* 105(2):171–192.

Peffley, Mark, Jon Hurwitz and Paul M. Sniderman. 1997. "Racial Stereotypes and Whites' Political Views of Blacks in the Context of Welfare and Crime." *American Journal of Political Science* 41(1):30–60.

Pérez, Efrén O. and Margit Tavits. 2019. "Language Influences Public Attitudes toward Gender Equality." *Journal of Politics* 81(1): 81–93.

Pérez, Efrén O. and Margit Tavits. 2022. *Voicing Politics: How Language Shapes Public Opinion*. Princeton: Princeton University Press.

Pettigrew, Thomas F. 2009. "Secondary Transfer Effect of Contact: Do Intergroup Contact Effects Spread to Noncontacted Outgroups?" *Social Psychology* 40: 55–65.

Pettigrew, Thomas F. and Linda R. Tropp. 2006. "A meta-analytic test of intergroup contact theory." *Journal of Personality and Social Psychology* 90(5): 751–783.

Rainey, Carlisle. 2014. "Arguing for a Negligible Effect." *American Journal of Political Science* 58(4): 1083–1091.

Sanbonmatsu, Kira. 2002. "Gender Stereotypes and Vote Choice." *American Journal of Political Science* 46(1): 20–34.

Schaffner, Brian F. 2022a. "Optimizing the Measurement of Sexism in Political Surveys." *Political Analysis* 30(3): 364–380.

Schaffner, Brian F. 2022b. "The Heightened Importance of Racism and Sexism in the 2018 US Midterm Elections." *British Journal of Political Science* 52(1): 492–500.

Schneider, Monica C. 2014. "The Effects of Gender-Bending on Candidate Evaluations." *Journal of Women, Politics & Policy* 35(1): 55–77.

Schneider, Monica C., Angela L. Bos and Madeline DiFilippo. 2022. "Gender Role Violations and Voter Prejudice: The Agentic Penalty Faced by Women Politicians." *Journal of Women, Politics & Policy* 43(2): 117–133.

Simonovits, Gábor, Gábor Kézdi and Péter Kardos. 2018. "Seeing the World through the Other's Eye: An Online Intervention Reducing Ethnic Prejudice." *American Political Science Review* 112(1): 186–193.

Tankard, Margaret E. and Elizabeth Levy Paluck. 2017. "The Effect of a Supreme Court Decision Regarding Gay Marriage on Social Norms and Personal Attitudes." *Psychological Science* 28(9): 1334–1344.

Tavits, Margit, Petra Schleiter, Jonathan Homola, and Dalston Ward. 2024. "Fathers' Leave Reduces Sexist Attitudes." *American Political Science Review* 118(1): 488–494.https://doi.org/10.1017/S0003055423000369.

Tavits, Margit and Efrén O. Pérez. 2019. "Language Influences Mass Opinion toward Gender and LGBT Equality." *Proceedings of the National Academy of Sciences* 116(34): 16781–16786.

Thompson, Jack. 2022. "Attitudes towards LGBT Individuals After Bostock v. Clayton County: Evidence From a Quasi Experiment." *Political Research Quarterly* 75(4): 1374–1385.

Valentino, Nicholas A. and Ted Brader. 2011. "The Sword's Other Edge: Perceptions of Discrimination and Racial Policy Opinion after Obama." *Public Opinion Quarterly* 75(2): 201–226.

Weber, Renee and Jennifer Crocker. 1983. "Cognitive Processes in the Revision of Stereotypic Beliefs." *Attitudes and Social Cognition* 45(5): 961–977.

West, Candace and Don H. Zimmerman. 1987. "Doing Gender." *Gender and Society* 1(2): 125–151.

Whitehead, Andrew L. 2014. "Male and Female He Created Them: Gender Traditionalism, Masculine Images of God, and Attitudes toward Same-Sex Unions." *Journal for the Scientific Study of Religion* 53(3): 479–496.

Zaller, John R. 1992. *The Nature and Origins of Mass Opinion*. New York: Cambridge University Press.

Zuo, Bin, Fangfang Wen, Miao Wang and Yang Wang. 2019. "The Mediating Role of Cognitive Flexibility in the Influence of Counter-Stereotypes on Creativity." *Frontiers in Psychology* 10(105): 1–11.

Cambridge Elements ☰

Gender and Politics

Tiffany D. Barnes
University of Kentucky

Tiffany D. Barnes is Professor of Political Science at the University of Kentucky. She is the author of *Women, Politics, and Power: A Global Perspective* (Rowman & Littlefield, 2007) and, award-winning, *Gendering Legislative Behavior* (Cambridge University Press, 2016). Her research has been funded by the National Science Foundation (NSF) and recognized with numerous awards. Barnes is the former president of the Midwest Women's Caucus and founder and director of the Empirical Study of Gender (EGEN) network.

Diana Z. O'Brien
Washington University in St. Louis

Diana Z. O'Brien is the Bela Kornitzer Distinguished Professor of Political Science at Washington University in St. Louis. She specializes in the causes and consequences of women's political representation. Her award-winning research has been supported by the NSF and published in leading political science journals. O'Brien has also served as a Fulbright Visiting Professor, an associate editor at *Politics & Gender*, the president of the Midwest Women's Caucus, and a founding member of the EGEN network.

About the Series

From campaigns and elections to policymaking and political conflict, gender pervades every facet of politics. Elements in Gender and Politics features carefully theorized, empirically rigorous scholarship on gender and politics. The Elements both offer new perspectives on foundational questions in the field and identify and address emerging research areas.

Cambridge Elements $\equiv$

Gender and Politics

Elements in the Series

In Love and at War: Marriage in Non-State Armed Groups
Hilary Matfess

Counter-Stereotypes and Attitudes Toward Gender and LGBTQ Equality
Jae-Hee Jung and Margit Tavits

A full series listing is available at: www.cambridge.org/EGAP

Printed in the United States
by Baker & Taylor Publisher Services